EQUITY 101

CULTURE

*This book is dedicated to my parents, John & Blanch Linton,
in recognition of the culture of excellence, opportunity, and fairness with
which they raised me. Growing up, I was mostly unaware of race, but
when I learned about racial inequity, I knew how to work towards equity
because of how I was raised: everyone deserves the god-given right to
experience excellence and opportunity, no matter who they are, what
they look like, nor where they come from—and it is my personal
responsibility to ensure a culture exists that empowers this right.*

—*Curtis Linton*

*To Eva, Dominic, and Maya: You are our present,
the future, and the work*

—*Bonnie Davis*

CULTURE

BOOK 2

CURTIS LINTON
BONNIE M. DAVIS

CORWIN
A SAGE Company

CORWIN
A SAGE Company

FOR INFORMATION:

Corwin

A SAGE Company

2455 Teller Road

Thousand Oaks, California 91320

(800) 233-9936

www.corwin.com

SAGE Publications Ltd.

1 Oliver's Yard

55 City Road

London EC1Y 1SP

United Kingdom

SAGE Publications India Pvt. Ltd.

B 1/I 1 Mohan Cooperative Industrial Area

Mathura Road, New Delhi 110 044

India

SAGE Publications Asia-Pacific Pte. Ltd.

3 Church Street

#10-04 Samsung Hub

Singapore 049483

Acquisitions Editor: Dan Alpert

Associate Editor: Kimberly Greenberg

Editorial Assistant: Heidi Arndt

Permissions Editor: Karen Ehrmann

Project Editor: Veronica Stapleton Hooper

Copy Editor: Matthew Sullivan

Typesetter: C&M Digitals (P) Ltd.

Proofreader: Wendy Jo Dymond

Indexer: Judy Hunt

Cover Designer: Rose Storey

Printed in the United States of America.

Library of Congress Cataloging-in-Publication Data

Linton, Curtis. Equity 101 : book 2 : culture / Curtis Linton, Bonnie M. Davis.

pages cm

Includes bibliographical references and index.

ISBN 978-1-4129-9731-7 (alk. paper)

1. Educational equalization—United States—Case studies. I. Title.

LC213.2.L563 2013

379.2'6—dc23   2013024747

This book is printed on acid-free paper.

SFI Certified Sourcing
www.sfiprogram.org
SFI-00453

13 14 15 16 17 10 9 8 7 6 5 4 3 2 1

Contents

Acknowledgments   vii

About the Authors   xi

Prologue   xiii

1.   **A School Culture of Equity**   1
    Apollo Middle School—Tucson, Arizona   2

2.   **The Equity Framework**   17
    Culturally Proficient Teachers   20
    Working Definition of Equitable Culture   22
    Equity Characteristics Within Culture   26
    The Equity Lens   27

3.   **Equitable Culture: Expectations**   33
    High Expectations: Belief Systems   36
    High Expectations: Culturally Proficient
       Communication Styles   38
    High Expectations: Educator Responsibility   40
    The Attitude of High Expectations   42

4.   **Equitable Culture: Rigor**   45
    Rigor Within Equity   47
    Defining Rigorous Culture   48
    Student Potential as Defined by Rigor   50
    Creating a Culture of Rigor   52

5.   **Equitable Culture: Relevancy**   57
    Relevant School Culture   59
    Inclusive Environment   60

Avoiding Disengagement   61
Culture of Relevancy   62
Cultural Competency   64
Respeto   66
Minimizing Whiteness   68

6. **Equitable Culture: Relationships**   **71**
Equitable Culture: Developing Relationships   72
Equitable Culture: Student Relationships   73
Equitable Culture: Collaboration   77
Equitable Culture: Parent and Community Relationships   79
Family Centers   80

7. **Equitable Culture: Actualization**   **85**

Epilogue   **103**

References   **105**

Index   **107**

Acknowledgments

First and foremost, I need to acknowledge Bonnie Davis for creating a collaborative culture where she allows me to stand in my strengths, despite my weaknesses. Thank you, Bonnie, for sticking with me during this long writing process—I could never hope for a better co-author.

I also thank my assistant, Megan Tolman, who keeps me busy, organized, and moving forward. I also thank my thought partner, Lisa Leith, who never lets an assumption simply stand on its own assumptions. Likewise, I thank the incredible content team members at School Improvement Network who strive every day to document on video and in print the very best in education.

Huge thanks needs to be expressed to my editor, Dan Alpert, the most patient, understanding, and supportive man I have ever worked with—thanks for sticking with me.

Without the hundreds of educators who have allowed me and my crew into their schools and classrooms, I never would have had the opportunity to learn about equity and effective school culture. The most important person in the work of school improvement is the ground-level practitioner who shows up every day ready to lead students toward their greatest hopes and aspirations—I honor and thank you all for the incredible work you do.

Most of all, I thank my wife, Melody, for keeping me humbled and focused on why this work really matters. Thanks.

—Curtis Linton

In 2004, Melody Linton handed my self-published book to Blanch Linton, who handed it to Corwin Press. Since then, I have had the wonderful opportunity of working with both the Linton family and

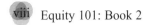

their company, School Improvement Network, as well as Corwin Press. I am grateful to all. At Corwin Press, I was assigned an editor, Dan Alpert, and in addition to being the best possible editor, he is a special friend. I am grateful for the support from Corwin staff: Heidi Arndt, Kim Greenberg, and Terra Schultz. A special thanks to Megan Tolman, assistant to Curtis, who has been especially helpful in bringing this project to fruition. Last, but most important of all, thanks to Curtis Linton, who gave me this opportunity to work with him. Working with Curtis has been a true gift in my life.

—Bonnie Davis

PUBLISHER'S ACKNOWLEDGMENTS

Corwin gratefully acknowledges the contributions of the following reviewers:

Elizabeth Alvarez, Principal
Chicago Public Schools
Chicago, IL

Jacqueline Berman, Retired Teacher
Lawrence Public Schools
Lawrence, MA

Judy Brunner, Clinical Faculty, Author, Consultant
Missouri State University & Instructional Solutions Group
Springfield, MO

David Freitas, Professor
Indiana University South Bend
Granger, IN

Roberta Glaser Carlsen, Assistant Superintendent of Schools (Retired)
St. Johns Public Schools
St. Johns, MI

Toni Jones, Superintendent
Falls Church City Public Schools
Falls Church, VA

Betty Porter Walls, Assistant Professor of Education
Harris-Stowe State University
St. Louis, MO

About the Authors

 **Curtis Linton** is executive vice president and co-owner of School Improvement Network, where he oversees all content and product development. The resources produced by Curtis and his team support administrators, principals, and teachers in increasing their effectiveness as educators so they can succeed in helping 100% of students become college and career ready. Throughout his career, Curtis has documented the improvement efforts and best practices of the most successful schools across North America. Annually, Curtis and his team visit over 100 of the very best classrooms and schools where equity is actualized every day.

Curtis has authored several books, including *Equity 101: The Equity Framework,* and co-authored *Courageous Conversations About Race: A Field Guide for Achieving Equity in Schools,* which received the 2006 National Staff Development Council's Book of the Year award. Curtis is also a nationally recognized education consultant specializing in equity, school improvement, leadership, and Common Core. In addition, he is a co-organizer of the national Summit for Courageous Conversations, an educational conference that focuses on building racial equity in schools.

Curtis lives with his wife, Melody, and two children, Dominic and Maya, in Salt Lake City, Utah. With his wife, he runs the Domino Foundation, which supports families that have adopted transracially. For more information, visit www.dominofoundation .org. He received his master's degree from the University of Southern California. Curtis can be reached through the School

Improvement Network at curtis.linton@schoolimprovement.com and www.schoolimprovement.com.

Photo by Kim Anderson.

Bonnie M. Davis, PhD, is a veteran teacher of more than 40 years who is passionate about education. She holds a BS in education, an MA in English, an MAI in communications and film studies, and a PhD in English. For 30 years, she taught English in secondary schools, community colleges, universities, homeless shelters, and a men's prison. Following that, she was the professional development program planner for the International Education Consortium, housed at the University of Missouri-St. Louis.

Dr. Davis is the recipient of many awards, including Teacher of the Year in two districts, the Anti-Defamation League's World of Difference Community Service Award, the Missouri Governor's Award for Teaching Excellence, and the 2012 Educational Innovator Award from the School Improvement Network.

Dr. Davis's Corwin Press books include *How to Teach Students Who Don't Look Like You: Culturally Responsive Teaching Strategies* (2nd ed., 2012), *How to Coach Teachers Who Don't Think Like You: Using Literacy Strategies to Coach Across Content Areas* (2007), *The Biracial and Multiracial Student Experience: A Journey to Racial Literacy* (2009), and *Creating Culturally Considerate Schools: Educating Without Bias* (2012, with co-author Kim L. Anderson). Other publications include numerous articles and book chapters focusing on literacy and equity.

Dr. Davis is the mother of two adult children, Leah and Reeve, and one granddaughter, Eva, and resides in St. Louis, Missouri with Fred Baugh, her partner of 22 years. She provides professional development services to districts, giving keynotes, workshops, and ongoing support through her consulting firm, Educating for Change. She may be reached at www.educatingforchange.com or by e-mail at a4achievement@earthlink.net.

Prologue

My wife and I bought our first house in a beautiful old neighborhood of craftsman bungalows in Salt Lake City, Utah. I love to cook, and I had always dreamed of growing tomatoes in my garden. I had never actually grown tomatoes, though I had pulled up thousands of weeds around my mother's plants when I was young. In all my enthusiasm, I looked at my yard and discovered that it was hard, dry, solid clay. It had been decades since any previous owner had worked and churned the soil. The clay was so hard that not even grass and weeds would grow in it.

My first thought was that I better buy a high-quality tomato plant for it to succeed in this hard, clayey soil—the extra money would be worth it to get the big, red, juicy tomatoes I dreamed of. Luckily, a patient and understanding person at the garden center kindly explained that if I did not rework the soil through tilling, aerating, and adding significant manure and organic material to it, the clay soil would choke my plant's roots and cause the plant to wither and die.

Before I ever planted a single tomato plant, I spent many hours and several weeks churning the soil in my yard and creating a system—a culture—that could not only keep alive what I planted, but also allow them to grow, thrive, and produce the beautiful fruits and vegetables I hoped to harvest. Harvesting this produce could only come after creating the ongoing conditions for effective growth and development.

School culture is like the soil that plants grow in. If, in a garden, we focus all of our efforts on watering, pruning, feeding, and supporting the plants without assuring the soil is ready, we are left with weak plants that wither and die at the slightest challenge. If, in a school, we focus all of our efforts on the strategies, curriculum, data, assessments, and interventions without first building a culture of acceptance, support, relationships, and excellence for each and every individual student and educator, then we keep the school on the cycle of continuous improvement without ever actually improving.

In visiting, observing, and documenting hundreds of highly successful schools across North America, I have strongly concluded that all of the "best practices" in education cannot overcome a toxic school culture accustomed to mediocre student performance. No matter how wealthy or poor, no matter how White or Brown or Black, no matter whether English is spoken as a first or second language, no matter whatever other characteristic may define a school—the success of the students and educators depends on the effort they put into building the culture of the school.

One year after our tomatoes started growing, we added life and soul to our beautiful little garden: We adopted our son, Dominic, and then four years later, we adopted our daughter, Maya. Both children are Black and were placed with us by their African American birth mothers. Even though Melody and I had worked hard to build a culture within our home that was loving, supportive, and accepting of everyone, we recognized that the "garden" of our own lives—our cultural competency—was insufficiently devoid of racial understanding and awareness. Much like our physical garden, we had to till our internal "soil" and enrich it with knowledge, relationships, and awareness of what it means to be of color in a very White world—we had to build a truly inclusive culture within our home where the inherent differences between us and our own children could be normed and equalized.

About the time Dominic was born, I met Bonnie Davis, one of my key allies and partners in this work of equitizing education for all students. Bonnie likewise is a White parent of a Black son. For me, she was one of the clearest voices I had ever heard as to what it means to acknowledge one's own Whiteness in an effort to overcome institutionalized inequities and racism—whether in school or in the home. Bonnie laid out the strategies, illustrated the realities, and helped me process the White side of racial equity. Through these conversations, I learned how to look at the privilege of my own White experience, rather than dwelling solely on the inequities of others different from myself.

I invite you to join me and my co-author Bonnie Davis on this journey to build an equitable school culture that works for all students.

Bonnie is one of the foremost educational experts on what it means to work through personal experience, bias, and expectations to succeed with students different from one's self. This is at the heart of creating an equitable school culture: norming difference for students so that each and every one fundamentally knows he or she is loved, accepted, and supported toward excellence, no matter how that student might differ from the educators and other students in the building. An equitable school culture can only exist when the staff as a whole is vested in creating an environment wherein every student succeeds.

Throughout this book, when we use the term *diverse* to describe students, we are referencing directly the racial and other characteristics that set apart a student from the dominant White and middle-class norms that have so defined the practices and culture of our schools. Serving one "norm" rather than the vast diversities now so apparent in today's students only guarantees the continuation of educational inequities. As educators work to directly address their school's racial and other inequities, they will accomplish equity, which is eliminating student achievement disparities and lifting all students to high levels of success.

For schools to achieve this, educators need to address equity at three levels: personal, institutional, and professional. The first book of this series, *Equity 101: The Equity Framework,* addressed these levels as follows:

- Personal equity guides the process of centering one's self in equity and uncovering one's own biases, stereotypes, and privileges.
- Institutional equity explores how a school and school system can overcome institutionalized factors that limit student achievement, especially for students of color and those from diverse backgrounds.
- Professional equity focuses on how efforts to successfully implement equitable practices can assure individualized support for all students.

Real stories of change are critically important in achieving equity. Throughout this book, we share the stories of schools, school systems, and educators who went through a change process personally, institutionally, and professionally to achieve equity for their students. These stories illustrate the process of equitizing education so that it works for all students, no matter their personal diversities.

Whether a teacher, a principal, a coach, or an administrator, these examples of real educators and actual schools serve as a model for you and your colleagues in creating an equitable culture that works for all students.

Throughout this book, we prompt you to use the equity lens as your tool in deciphering the equity efforts of the educators in these stories—and ultimately in understanding your own efforts to equitize your work as an educator. At the end of each chapter, engage in the Equity in Action implementation exercises, which include discussion questions and reflection prompts. Further, you will be guided to take advantage of the School Improvement Network's on-demand professional development resource, PD 360, where you will find interactive forums and videos of the schools in this book, and engage the *Educator Effectiveness System* as an ongoing support in your equity efforts. To access these tools, please visit www.school improvement.com/equity101.

No individual student ever enters school with the hope to fail. The natural inclination for a student is to dream of excellence and acceptance. But when school culture stands between the student and his or her dreams, the school has failed in its fundamental purpose of helping all kids succeed. Equitable school culture is the foundational characteristic of educational institutions that work day in, day out for adults and students alike. Thank you for entering into this journey with us to norm difference in our schools for all kids.

Sincerely,

Curtis Linton

CHAPTER 1

A School Culture of Equity

What is a school culture of equity? A school culture of equity is a fostered and cultivated attitude, expectation, and understanding of where students need to be and how to get them there. A school culture of equity is one where educators create a classroom, school, and system where excellence is achieved for every student, no matter who that student is or where that student comes from. In a school culture of equity, diversity becomes the norm, not the exception, and excellence becomes the norm for all, not the exception for a few. No matter how different and diverse the individual's background and characteristics might be, the equitable school culture embraces the uniqueness, strengths, and challenges of the student and provides equitable support, understanding, expectations, and encouragement to succeed. Equity can only occur in a culture where it is safe for adults and students alike to take risks, stretch, learn, and authentically engage day in, day out. In a school where this is possible, faculty hold themselves to the highest expectations and professional responsibility, while doing what is necessary to understand themselves and their students racially and culturally. In a school culture of equity, excellence and success become the norm for each student and every educator. In this book, you will meet educators who meet these qualifications and who engage in equity. The stories in this book, and the videos that accompany it, are those of real teachers in real classrooms. This is not a book of theory; this is a book of practice.

This book offers you a framework for examining school cultures of equity and the equity actions necessary to norm excellence and success for all. Written for administrators, teacher leaders, coaches, and pre-service teachers, this book provides you with models of equity as well as a framework to use to address equity in your school. In addition, in using this book, you gain access to an online community of educators where you can discuss videos of the successful schools described throughout the book. By joining the online community, you are engaging in a Equity 101 Book Study that is dynamic, live, and energizing—a powerful antidote to the possible boredom, invisibility, and hopelessness that might lurk behind a closed teacher's door. Your voice is as important as every other voice, including ours, the authors, and you have the power to contribute and mold the ongoing conversation; so relax, delve into the book, and please join us for the online conversations based on the questions at the end of each chapter. Enjoy!

Apollo Middle School—Tucson, Arizona

Driving up to Apollo Middle School, evidence that this school sits in one of the toughest neighborhoods in Tucson, Arizona surrounds you. Potholed roads. Dirt sidewalks. Dilapidated homes. Bars on all windows. Police patrols. And intimidating fences surrounding the school and the homes surrounding it. But this image belies what has happened within Apollo Middle School. In four year's time, under the direction of Principal Ray Chavez, Apollo went from state takeover to the top 10% of all middle schools in Arizona. Yes, this was accomplished with great leadership. And yes, this was accomplished by changing the practices teachers apply with students everyday. But most impactfully, Apollo achieved this success because it fundamentally changed the culture of the school to rigorously support the students in a culturally relevant way.

In his office, Principal Chavez points to a piece of student art hanging on his wall, a crayon drawing of the character Eeyore from Winnie the Pooh, and says, "That Eeyore was given to me by an eighth grader the year before I got here." It is a photocopied worksheet of a line drawing of the forlorn donkey from Winnie the Pooh. It has blue crayon messily scribbled all over the picture. With firm conviction, Ray continues:

Coloring Eeyore in eighth grade is an absolute insult to that kid, to the parent, to our teaching profession. Any kind of way you want to describe it, a kid's insulted that way. No wonder the place was crazy! It's a logical extension of that kind of treatment to kids that the kids treat you the same way back.

Apollo Middle School was locked in a perpetual state of failure that not only killed the potential of the kids, but also impacted the morale of the teachers. Eeyore became a symbol for Ray of what Apollo fundamentally could not be:

Most people think it's just a silly thing. But I keep it there as a reminder to me we're never going there. If I find a teacher doing that, I will do whatever I have to do to make sure they're gone.

On arriving four years earlier, Principal Chavez joined forces with his assistant principal, Lorena Martinez. They established a BHAG—a *Big Hairy Audacious Goal*—that within four years they would reach "Highly Performing" status, which in Arizona would place them within the top 10% of all middle schools. Ray recounts that when he would attend administrative meetings and share Apollo's BHAG, other administrators "snickered" and thought, "You're just crazy."

Ray was driven by a mission to succeed with Latino kids just like him. He grew up in the Sunnyside neighborhood not far from the school he was now leading. His wife taught in one of the feeder elementary schools and repeatedly expressed frustration in preparing younger children to have a chance, only to see them enter Apollo, get lost in the shuffle, and fall precipitously behind—almost as if the school was "preparing them to drop out." Throughout his life, Ray had been involved in Chicano movements and had been an activist for change, even gaining notoriety as a member of the Mexican Studies team in neighboring Tucson Unified School District. His wife pushed him to get even more intentional about driving school change:

She told me, "Mr. Chicano, go and put your money where your mouth is. Take that school, and go do something with it." The place was crazy. I mean there are not very many other words you can use to describe it. It was out of hand.

Beginning in the summer of 2007, the first task in front of Principal Chavez and his new administrative team was building the capacity of the teaching staff. Announcing the BHAG to the staff, Ray defined it in terms of equitable opportunity for the students of Apollo:

> If I were to attempt to define equity for us, it's that access to opportunity for every one of my kids. Sometimes our kids in their life situation struggle a lot, and it's not any fault of their own. We need to try to make a place where if you come here and do your very best, things can change . . . If we have access to opportunities—I had a degree, a BA, an MA from the University of Arizona, another Master's degree from Harvard. I have opportunities. How can I get you [the student] in a position where you can exercise opportunities?

After laying out the performance goals and expectations of the teaching and support staff, more than 40% of the Apollo teachers either resigned or requested a transfer to another school—they simply did not believe the students of Apollo were capable of such high achievement. He even had one teacher who entered his office, handed in his resignation, abruptly said, "I will never work for a Mexican," turned, and walked out the door. Their work was cut out for them.

Having to quickly hire almost 40 teachers over the summer to a school with a bad reputation of gangs and poor performance, Ray and his team knew they would not find Teacher of the Year–type veteran candidates. But what they could find were teachers who cared deeply for the students. They determined that it was far easier to train a teacher to teach effectively than to care deeply. Assistant Principal Lorena Martinez remembers collectively believing, "It's not going to be easy, but we're going to do this . . . we have a moral imperative to do this for this community."

To move the focus of the students back on academics, Apollo instituted a number of positive behavior programs, including recognizing students with awards and rewards, pairing students with significant adults, and moving gang-prevention efforts from a "law enforcement" activity to a focus on alternate social and academic opportunities. All of this was paired with a significant increase in academic expectations for each and every student.

According to Principal Chavez, Apollo discovered a simple way to approach discipline with students:

> We have lots of rules, but the one real rule is the *nana* rule. The nana rule is if your nana [grandmother] was standing right behind you, what would you do, or what actions and decisions would you make if she was standing right behind you, what would those be like? Every kid tells you the same thing. They'd be great. They'd be good because they're honoring their parents and their grandparents and so on. So that is an example of their culture manifesting itself in what we do here at the school. If you follow that rule, you're going to make gold and the kids get that.

This effort required a substantial amount of professional development, coaching, and teacher support. But the teachers quickly begin applying the new practices and expectations in the classroom, improving their effectiveness year after year. Principal Chavez described to the teachers how "[k]ids like to be challenged. They want it. If you pitch too low, they know when they're insulted. If you pitch too high, they get frustrated, but they've got to be in that reach." Educators focused on their strengths while incorporating new student-engagement practices. Teacher Kathy Mayorga says,

> My style of teaching is still the same. It's very structured. But I do lot more group work, a lot more accountability of the students, a lot of projects, incorporating the skills into projects, keeping the students actively engaged, and making it fun for the students.

Likewise, professional development focused on helping teachers provide intriguing and rigorous instruction. As students became more engaged and focused on the rigor, classroom management improved, and teachers began honoring the learning interests and readiness of individual students, an interesting phenomenon occurred, as described by Ray: "The rigor part creates relationships. The kids should be asking, 'I'm having a hard time here. Help me.'" With improved relationships tied to increased rigor, teacher–student conversations became the norm. According to teacher Kathy Mayorga,

> Teachers are out and visible talking to students. Students are accepting of that and are not afraid to ask for help, whether it's

with the problem they're having at home, or it's a problem in school, or a problem with the work. It's also the teachers' attitudes changing—being here for students since the students are number one.

Within the first year, their effort started to have an impact. The staff had shifted from managing students to driving their academic achievement. The belief in the students' potential became palpable, and enthusiasm grew for the goals established by Ray. According to Assistant Principal Tammy Christopherson, it truly was the heart and commitment of the teachers that kept them on track for the BHAG through the first year:

> We had very, very low skills actually with the teachers. But what we did have was heart. We had teachers who just wanted to be here. We had teachers who wanted to see it succeed. I think just the work ethic alone was pretty phenomenal and that energy just carried.

Apollo's initial focus and eventual success was built on creating cultural relevance for students. Principal Chavez states that "[l]ots of times schools approach education in a single model and our kids are not a single model." Since kids were individually unsuccessful, Apollo needed to build a culturally relevant educational experience that individual students could connect with. According to Lorena Martinez, "When you tap into what a kid knows and his experiences, that's relevancy. And it's engaging and it's relevant to them and it takes what they come with into consideration, and the kids get into it."

But cultural relevance in schools has had numerous iterations with varying degrees of success—multiculturalism, native language studies, historical and cultural focus on students' country of origin, culture celebrations, and so on. At Apollo, cultural relevance was defined as education that relates to the student's local and immediate experience. This could include references to country of origin, cultural traditions, language, and histories, but within the context of how this is experienced by the student day by day. Apollo's cultural relevance efforts also tapped into local current events, members of the community, and the student's own family to define what mattered to the student.

At the beginning of his teaching career, Ray Chavez discovered by accident the power of relevant instruction focused on the immediate, local, and cultural experience of the student:

> I was a rookie teacher. I got hired in '82 in this building at Apollo Middle School. And my classroom was not your typical classroom. I didn't know what I was doing, and the kids are just running around making all kinds of mayhem in the classroom. I was reduced to guarding the door to make sure they didn't escape and go somewhere else to make problems. It was around the third week of October which means Halloween is around the corner, and the kids are starting to think about that. These two little girls are sitting right in front of me with the rest of the room in mayhem, and they asked me if I believed in ghosts. When I said, "No, there's no such thing," they looked down disappointed. Then I jumped in with, "But La Llorona is a whole different thing." And they perked up because they've never heard La Llorona discussed in a schoolhouse before—at home, yes, but never at school.

La Llorona translates into "The Weeping Woman," and is a widespread legend across Mexico and in Latino cultures of the American Southwest. The basic story is that a woman named Maria lost her children by drowning. She wanders around at night near bodies of water crying, "Ay, mis hijos! Ay, mis hijos!" which translates to "Oh, my children!" La Llorona is widely used in Latino culture as a cautionary tale for kids.

> So we started talking about La Llorona. They called another kid up to join us. And so now the four of us are talking about this thing that they hear at home, and other stories and folktales that they're told at home from their parents or grandparents. We very quickly got involved in that discussion pretty deeply.
>
> Then I looked around the room. Just a couple minutes before, this room had just been out of control, which was typical, but was now dead quiet. All the kids in the room were focused, pin drop quiet, which is not typical.
>
> Well, pretty soon the bell rang. They were disappointed because the fun is over. But I told them, "Go home. Talk to your

folks. We're going to write it down, and then tomorrow in class we'll read them and share more." So they thought that was great. I didn't know what was going to happen that night. I was lying in bed thinking about it and wondering what will happen because I had begun to believe what people had told me about these kids.

The next day when the kids arrived at school waving their papers in their hands, I quickly read some of them. They were well composed. All the pieces of literature we've been trying to teach were in there. And that's the day I found out what was missing: the connection from their home to school, and in this case, it happened to be their culture!

So we studied La Llorona—that spectral presence that haunts waterways. We looked at waterways all around Arizona. I was being paid to teach Arizona history. So we examined how that story is told in any town in Arizona. We got the history of Arizona, the geography of Arizona. We got all the state standards, but we did it in a way that the kids thought was fun—it was a presentation method of the teaching that they understood. They had already learned it at home, so that mediation between their home culture and the school culture [was natural].

I was warned by some of the other teachers, "Better knock it off. These kids are not going to be able to pass that test." We had to pass the Arizona History test here in Arizona for eighth graders to get out of the eighth grade. My kids just crushed it because they learned very deeply in a different context!

Assistant Principal Lorena Martinez recalls the impact Ray had on his students when he made the shift to culturally relevant instruction. "All of a sudden he had every kid turned around. The entire attention of those kids was on Mr. Chavez because all of a sudden, they were talking about something that was relevant to them."

"If they don't see a value of what you're teaching them in their lives, they're not going to buy into it and make that effort to learn," says social studies teacher Steve Olguin. "So if you can make the things that they are supposed to learn relative to their daily lives, you're succeeding and you're respecting their culture." He has readdressed his whole curriculum so that it is culturally relevant for the students.

We were able to do that basically by getting to know the students better, getting to know their families better, and speaking individually to the mother and father. That really helped us understand the type of student that we are working with.

Another social studies teacher, Jennifer Trujillo-Johnson, says, "I don't assign anything that wouldn't be relevant to them in some way." She reads from their heritage, folk tales, and current events. The students respond with pride to these stories: "Hey, this came from Mexico." "This came from the southwest—that's where I'm from!" "Hey I've heard that story." "My nina told me that story, that's cool!" "That story came from my culture." Jennifer describes great success with these approaches because it taps into the prior knowledge of the students. Lorena Martinez reaffirms this in describing that the students "Know who they are. They know where they come from. The fact that we validate that validates themselves."

This approach extends into the standards taught in the classroom. According to Mr. Olguin,

Anything that you teach be it the state standards or if they were national standards, you have to relate it to their personal lives. Otherwise if they don't see a value of what you're teaching them in their lives, they're not going to buy into it and make that effort to learn.

For one unit studying the waves of European immigrants from the late 1890s to the early 1930s, he compared it to modern immigration—a relevant issue for these Arizona students who live less than 50 miles from the Mexican border, and most of whom are children of immigrants:

As you know, immigration is a hot topic here in Arizona. So while we're studying the immigration issues of the late 1800s and early 1900s, we related it to the immigration problems we have now . . . So we're learning the past but we're also looking at today, the issues of today. And we're trying to contrast them or find similarities between them. And surprisingly, a lot of the issues that were happening in the past are the same issues that we're having today.

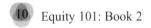

Trujillo-Johnson builds on these themes in her own class:

We read about border violence that's happening along the Mexican–U.S. border. And it was one of my most successful articles that I've done with them because it relates to a lot of them. I had one kid that's moved from El Paso to here to escape the violence. One kid's uncle was tortured. It was a lot of stories that were coming out and a really high interest piece of information for the class to get involved with.

Mr. Olguin continues, saying,

If you can make the things that they are supposed to learn relative to their daily lives, you're succeeding and you're respecting their culture. So I think that relativeness makes it personal for the students and what they are learning. How is it going to help you today? How is it going to help you in life in the future? They buy into that.

This culturally relevant approach addresses a wider context than what is addressed in the textbook because it approaches learning directly based on what the students already understand. "This is about treating people with dignity and respect," describes Martinez. "How much more dignity and respect than to dignify where they come from and what they know and bring it from there?"

Prior to Apollo Middle School's turnaround, there were limited relationships with the community. Students entered the gates of the school, but parents rarely ventured in. The staff discovered that it wasn't a lack of interest in their children's education on the part of the community. Rather, most parents came from Mexican and Central American communities where the cultural norm was to maintain a deferential relationship of respect toward the teacher, rather than to engage the teacher in personal dialogue about the child.

What Apollo realized was that parents needed educational and instructional services to successfully support their child through middle and high school, and on to college. Since the ultimate goal was to support student achievement, and parent engagement was critical in pulling this off, the staff at Apollo created an evening *Community School.* According to Principal Chavez,

It's [about] how you get the community involved in supporting the school and what happens in the school. The goal is to have Dad at a financing college work class, Mom down in a fitness room, the daughter working on the computer, and maybe the oldest son giving some tutoring lessons to elementary kids. The conversation on Saturday morning is probably going to be about Apollo Middle School and how it's an important piece of the entire community.

Since funding is limited at Apollo, there were not significant financial resources to put into parent and community support. Through grants, volunteers, and relying on resources already in place, Apollo created a robust parent and community program that included the following:

– Opening the computer lab with full Internet access to parents at night—this came after discovering most community members were waiting in long lines to share only two computer terminals at the local library

– Conducting computer and Internet literacy classes for parents

– Providing fitness classes and access after hours for parents and their children to the school's exercise room and gym

– Hosting workshops conducted by community service organizations, such as English language classes

– Providing after-hours tutoring for students, and training parents in how to support their children's homework

– Establishing a local law enforcement liaison at the school to work with parents

– Creating a college education course which introduces parents to the many facets of the U.S. college and university system, including

  o application procedures
  o college entrance exams
  o scholarships, student aid, and FAFSA application
  o introductions to local, state, and national vocational programs, junior colleges, and universities
  o field trips to local college and university campuses

The college preparedness class has been one of the most popular services offered at Apollo. Once, right before a field trip to the University of Arizona campus for students and parents, a student who was particularly interested in the visit suddenly said he could not participate. The student told the advisor that he could not attend because he and his parents did not have official permits to walk on the campus. Hearing that anyone is allowed to enter the campus, the student and his parents were relieved and excited to visit the university—the first time anyone in the family had ever visited a university campus.

The Community School has been very popular with parents and students alike. The goals at Apollo are always focused on increasing academic achievement, and the Community School has become a primary vehicle to empower the community in supporting the students. According to Chavez, "That's kind of the driving force behind it, making our kids academic beings, and them understanding themselves being academic beings in this community."

With parents and students alike, Apollo pushes a program called PASFUE: *Preparing All Students for University Enrollment.* The program focuses on helping students develop habits of mind and study, as well as the necessary attitudes so that students develop a college path within their minds. Consequently, the school ends up being a provider of options rather than a terminal experience. "Kids weren't being provided options like that through the school," describes Principal Chavez.

> That's a huge thing. That is a giant. Once a kid understands the options and you give them hope to accomplish options, get out of the way because once the kids are on that path, they understand why we're pushing."

The students readily speak to the changes that have occurred at Apollo Middle School. Eighth-grade student Rafael describes his school:

> Before you would talk about Apollo and others would say, "Oh, it's a fighting school. Oh, they don't have anything good in there. Oh, it's all bad. I don't know why you go there." And now, we want to prove to them that Apollo is the best. So we're trying our hardest to make it the best.

Students naturally strive for excellence. Academic success happens when students see that the school is fully aligned with their own drive for achievement. As described by Ray, "It just seemed like the kids were waiting for somebody to tell them, 'You're smart and you're good,' because those are the two things that we had a reputation of being: not smart and being bad."

Apollo has moved from perennially failing to one of the top performing middle schools in Arizona. This is based on the increase in AIMS, the *Arizona Instrument to Measure Success,* scores. The educators took it to the students, as described by Principal Chavez:

> I told the kids, "Look where we are. If you're happy with this thing, you're going to have problems here because we're not going to be staying here. We're going to go up." And so the first year, we went from underperforming year two status, past year one, passed underperforming, and then we got to performing status the first year. The second year we went to performing plus status, except on the low end of that scale. Last year, we went to performing plus status on the high end of that scale, and just missed highly performing status by one point in the measurement!

In four years' time, not only had Apollo Middle School shed its failing status, but it had also climbed to nearly the highest ranking of Arizona schools. It is a remarkable achievement that has not gone without notice—or without doubt. As described by Samantha, an eighth-grade student,

> When we went from failing to performing they had like all this FBI people coming in here, and checking on the kids, and making sure they were doing it right, and that they weren't cheating and stuff. And they had that going on like the entire time there was AIMS. And the next year, they just left it alone because they knew that we were doing everything right, and that we were just literally excelling towards better!

Apollo is proof that demographics and perennial failure do not have to stand in the way of substantial student achievement gains. When educators fully commit to modify the school in every way necessary, improve their instructional practices, and make learning culturally relevant, students readily connect with the increased rigor, trust the relationships with educators, and excel in their academic performance. Alexis, a student at Apollo, testifies to this: "It feels like they care. And they do want you to understand what they are teaching."

Ray Chavez describes what Apollo has done as radical and at the front line of civil rights activism:

> I used to be an almost militant activist in terms of the Chicano and Mexican-American community. I was involved in a lot of things that would be considered pushing that envelope a lot. But this right here might be the most radical thing I've done because people expect kids to fail here. We're not supposed to be having these kinds of results. And that other thing of wanting to do good for your community in almost this radical way—I don't know if you could find a more radical thing to do than to flip this school completely on its head, and go put it in people's faces that these kids can excel at any kind of level!

The equitable culture of a school matters to its educators, parents, the community, and especially to its students. When the culture of a school focuses on developing high expectations, rigorous instruction and engagement for each and every student, cultural relevance in terms of what students learn, and strong connected relationships between teacher and student, there is no limit to how far a school can progress. When it works well—when a school is like the well-cultivated soil in a productive garden—school culture can overcome any limiting factor and succeed with any demographic difference brought by the student. The best schools are not those with perfect practice, but rather those that have created an environment where every student and every educator is supported in taking risks to grow, and is understood and fully accepted for whoever he or she is—no matter how wonderfully diverse the individual might be. This is the power of equitable school culture: the power of excellence in education.

Principal Ray Chavez summarizes the work by stating, "I don't know if you could find a more radical thing to do than to flip this thing completely on its head and go put it in people's faces that these kids can excel at any kind of level." The change in school culture that he and his staff accomplished at Apollo Middle School demonstrates what a group of educators can do when they engage in the seemingly radical act of simply achieving excellence for all students.

Equity Terms

To fully execute an equitable environment, it is necessary to have both common languages and practices among the staff in a school. Following are key terms and definitions that can guide your studies in this book and also in your personal and institutional professional development.

Equity: Justice, fairness, and freedom from bias or favoritism

Race: The color of one's skin; different from racism, which is prejudice based on skin color, and institutionalized racism, which is prejudice plus power

Diverse: Characteristics that differ from the majority norm, especially in terms of race, gender, economics, language, and culture

Culture of Equity: An environment wherein individuals are provided with what each personally needs in terms of resources and support, rather than receiving equal portions regardless of need

Equitize: Deliberate effort to shift an inequitable environment or situation toward equity rather than simply making things equal

Equity Lens: Analyzing a belief, situation, or action using equity as a basis for understanding

Equity Action: Defined action or engagement that builds equity within a culture and/or environment

Cultural Competency: Understanding the background, values, norms, and characteristics of one's own culture and the culture of others

Equity Discussion

Chapter 1 shares the story of profound school culture change at Apollo Middle School. Throughout this chapter, you read about the steps that Principal Ray Chavez and his staff took to accomplish this

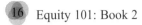

change. Please engage in the following activities to analyze equity according to what Principal Chavez and his staff accomplished, and how that compares to your own work.

Online PD 360 conversations:

- How would you describe what occurred at Apollo Middle School?
- How does your school foster or not foster student achievement?
- What works, what doesn't, and what is being done to develop a culture of high achievement at your school?

_____

_____

Equity Lens: Professional

Describe your professional challenges in terms of supporting all diverse students.

_____

_____

EQUITY ACTION #1

What challenge might you address first? What actions might you take?

_____

_____

CHAPTER 2

The Equity Framework

"Your voice is a part of this school no matter what you speak," exclaims Sandy Nobles, principal of J. Erik Jonsson Elementary School in Dallas, Texas. Sandy walks her talk and puts into practice what she preaches. The work in her building is no cliché: She and her staff work hard to maintain and grow an equitable school culture where every voice is heard and valued and where everyone is excited to be a part of the culture. Sandy describes this as energy: "[It] feels so right when it works, and [school's] a great place to spend a day. You're with people that like the work they're doing. You're with children excited about coming to school and learning." Building this school culture is a journey comprising many steps, and the equity framework illustrated herein offers a guide for taking that journey.

How does a teacher create a truly inclusive class where all students not only feel accepted fully for who they are, but also feel compelled to achieve excellence? Most all educators *strive* to create a learning environment where students feel safe and academically engaged. But this does not always happen. Creating an equitable academic culture is tricky business, requiring the successful confluence of many factors: the personal optimism and belief in the students embraced by the educator, the standard of excellence held by the academic institution, and the professional skills exhibited daily by the teacher in the classroom. But creating this equitable culture goes far beyond just chance—it requires the deliberate execution of a positive learning environment coupled with the cultural competency of the educator.

This book is about creating a culture of equity within academic institutions so that school works for all students, no matter who they are or where they come from. This book is part of the Equity 101 series and examines the *culture* component of the equity framework, as illustrated here, which was introduced in the first book, *The Equity Framework.*

To effect academic success for all students, equitable *culture* sets the stage for engagement and learning while working in trifecta with focused instructional *leadership* and effective teaching *practice,* the focus of the other two books in the series. Combined together, equitable leadership, culture, and practice can create a powerful school environment focused on high achievement for all students.

Equity is not about *equal* treatment of students, but *equal*—and thus *equitable*—educational results. With equity, all students—no

Figure 2.1   The Equity Framework

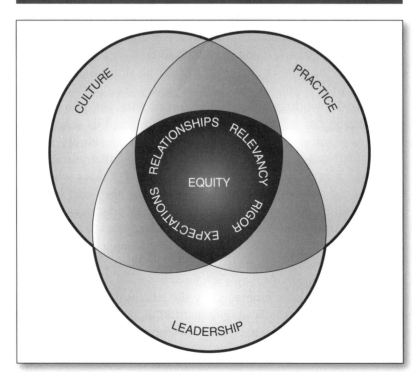

exceptions—are guaranteed success in school. But what is equity? As defined in *Equity 101: The Equity Framework,* educational equity occurs when *educators provide all students with the individual support they need to reach and exceed a common standard.* When equity occurs, each and every student receives individualized teaching and focused support based on the student's own readiness level and learning needs. The school does not end its effort in regard to the individual student until he or she has met and even exceeded the minimal academic achievement level as expected by the educational institution.

In the United States, the Common Core Standards define this minimally expected academic achievement level. The Common Core defines the standards as college and career readiness—a remarkably equitable definition. If the goal of K–12 education is to prepare students for life and for whatever may lie beyond their education, then college and career readiness becomes an admirable and measurable goal. No school can guarantee that all students will succeed in life, but all schools can guarantee that every student is prepared at high school graduation with the necessary skills and knowledge sets to enter college or advanced career training, ready to succeed. An institutionalized academic goal of college and career readiness provides all students with the choice to do whatever they want in life—the student gets to choose for him- or herself and does not face limited options due to inadequate preparation by the academic institution. This is fundamentally equitable because it expects schools to achieve a common outcome with all students rather than simply provide a common point of entry. When a school's efforts focus on achieving equity for all, then students are individually supported within their unique differences so as to achieve a more equal outcome.

Furthermore, this lofty equity goal of preparing all students to be ready to succeed at college, career, and beyond is admirable and fulfills the purpose of why most educators become teachers in the first place: to fundamentally impact the lives of the children they work with. But educational equity can only be achieved in a school culture that supports this goal—not only for students, but for educators as well. Successful educational practitioners Anthony Muhammad and Sharroky Hollie (2012) define school culture as a system, stating that "students are part of a school system—not a one-room schoolhouse," and their academic achievement mirrors the "collective will" of the educators in that institution (p. 10). Throughout their book, you will find examples of educators who have the "will and the skill" to educate children and who have developed the equitable culture necessary for that to occur. In defining equitable culture in schools, it is necessary to look at two primary components:

- *A Culture of Learning:* The school is a place that facilitates instructional innovation and rigorous learning, expects measurable growth, encourages exploration of learning and practice, and safely supports individual students and teachers alike in stretching and taking the necessary risks for success.
- *Cultural Competency:* Educators come to understand and support themselves and their students in terms of culture, race, ethnicity, gender, language, economics, and background by teaching in culturally relevant ways, engaging in courageous conversations, exploring race and difference, examining internal biases, and challenging institutionalized inequities.

These two components intricately work together in the classroom and the school. If a teacher can deeply connect with a student because he or she understands that student, and this connection takes place within a positive learning environment, the student is bound to engage and eventually succeed with the learning. Eli Gonzalez, a student at Apollo Middle School, says, "If the teachers see you're about to give up, they won't let you give up, because you'll end up having to try, and it will eventually pay off."

CULTURALLY PROFICIENT TEACHERS

The featured educators in this Equity 101 series mirror this combination of cultural competency plus culture of learning. They learn about themselves and about their students; they focus on the culture and environment in their classrooms—and they clearly understand that they are on a continual journey to understand culture and norm difference. Teachers throughout this series who demonstrate cultural proficiency and share similar attributes include the following:

Mike Hayes, math teacher at Amherst Middle School, Amherst, Massachusetts:

Mike clearly understands the different needs of his students. All his kids get modifications; they read word problems out loud together and solve math problems through an inquiry group process. They have identified two needs in math: the need to use numeracy in all subjects and the need for a student support class. During the support class, they provide help with homework, reinforce concepts, and immerse students in number games. The math teachers meet with the other teachers during their lunch periods and catch up on what each student needs.

Tracy Hudson, supervisor of elementary education at Indian River Elementary, Indian River, Delaware:

Tracy says that in their award-winning school, every child has a learning plan, similar to an IEP, and that has made a really big difference. No child could slip through the cracks, and teachers can learn about each child as an individual and truly understand them. They offer the students such things as before- and after-school help, mentoring, and individualized learning supports while being careful not to over-program any student.

Michele Lamon, English and American Sign Language (ASL) teacher at Pinole Valley High School, Richmond, California:

Michele uses rhythm and movement to engage each student in the work. No student is left alone; each must participate—and Michele's commanding presence sees that the class moves to a fast beat. Students are excited about learning ASL because once they enter the room, they are swept up into the energy of Michele's instruction. Michele is African American; her students are both culturally similar and culturally different. She norms difference by using ASL to be the controlling motif in her room, and her expectations are that each high school student will master the language. In 2010, Michelle was chosen as district Teacher of the Year.

These teachers share similar culturally competent characteristics:

- They teach in a way that connects to the cultures of their students.
- They hold high expectations and expect all students to achieve.

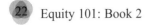

- They do not let any student "check out" of learning.
- They offer a support plan for all students.
- They keep the class lively, interesting, rigorous, and fun.

What makes their instruction culturally proficient and responsive? These teachers provide a clear focus on students and provide culturally competent instruction to ensure that all students achieve at high levels and reach mastery.

WORKING DEFINITION OF EQUITABLE CULTURE

Apollo Middle School illustrates a powerful example of what equitable school culture looks like when successfully implemented. But effective school culture is not simply an atmosphere in the school that everyone "gets along." Rather, it is a fostered and cultivated attitude, expectation, and understanding of where students need to be and how to get them there.

Observing hundreds of schools across North America that illustrate strong examples of highly effective, supportive, and rigorous academic environments has lead us to a working definition of equitable culture: *Schools create and maintain a rigorous, supportive, and inclusive learning environment that fully values each individual student and educator for who they are, where they come from, and what they can accomplish.* Supportive and inclusive school culture does not happen by chance. It requires diligent effort by educators examining their personal belief system and practices in collaboration with other educators. Furthermore, equitable school culture takes time and diligent refinement to work successfully for all students. A successful school is always *building* equitable culture rather than just *having* an equitable culture. Just like a vegetable garden can never be left on its own to produce a bountiful harvest, schools only achieve success by constantly focusing effort on building a culture that works with each and every student.

The first book of this series, *Equity 101: The Equity Framework,* defined personal, institutional, and professional equity as follows:

- *Personal Equity* guides you through the process of centering yourself in equity and uncovering your own biases, stereotypes, and privileges.

- *Institutional Equity* explores how your school and school system can overcome institutionalized factors that limit student achievement, especially for students of color and those from diverse backgrounds.
- *Professional Equity* focuses your efforts on successfully implementing equitable practices so as to assure individualized support for all students.

To fully illustrate this for both students and educators, visualize the working definition of equitable school culture when effectively implemented at the personal, institutional, and professional levels (see Table 2.1).

By analyzing equitable school culture on the personal, institutional, and professional levels, educators can quickly identify where

Table 2.1 Equitable Culture

Equitable Culture: Personal	
Educators	*Students*
• Each educator understands him- or herself personally according to race, gender, ethnicity, language, socio-economics, and home background—and how these characteristics impact his or her values, assumptions, biases, expectations, and relationships with students. • Each educator carries within him- or herself strong convictions as to the learning capacity of the students and the necessity to realize this potential—only success for each and every student is acceptable, as failure is not an option with any child.	• Each student is understood and valued for who he or she is personally according to race, gender, ethnicity, language, socioeconomics, and home background—and how these characteristics potentially impact the student's social and academic experience. • Students personally feel the high expectations, belief, and hope that the educators have for them—the student's academic and social strengths and weaknesses are regularly highlighted and tied to the life potential of the student.

(Continued)

(Continued)

Equitable Culture: Institutional	
Educators	*Students*
• The school systematically dismantles institutional inequities so as to eliminate predictable gaps or barriers to achievement according to student demographics and backgrounds—this includes revising formal policies, assessing traditions, making social norms inclusive for all, providing multiple language support, and collectively engaging in courageous conversations. • The school consciously and deliberately builds a supportive learning culture that works for educators and students alike—this includes creating safe risk-taking environments where teachers can try new approaches, developing true collaboration where educators can rely on each other to improve on weaknesses and share strengths, and developing evaluation structures that support and drive growth in teacher effectiveness.	• Students and their parents feel and know that the school and all its staff accept them for who they are, what they come with, and what they represent, regardless of student difference from the norm—teams, activities, clubs, leadership, and all classes, including general ed, advanced, honors, and remedial are fully inclusive and reflect the overall student demographic of the school. • Regardless of who the students are or where they come from, each and every student knows that the school and all its teachers hold them to the highest standard of excellence and achievement—this includes providing the individualized support, learning flexibility, safety for risk taking, and relevancy based on student needs so that each student can progress ever upward in his or her academic and social achievement.
Equitable Culture: Professional	
Educators	*Students*
• Teachers, coaches, and support staff regularly employ culturally relevant curriculum and learning strategies so that students	• On a day-by-day basis, students engage in relevant curriculum that reflects their immediate reality, personal experience, and cultural

Equitable Culture: Institutional	
Educators	*Students*
see themselves in their learning and clearly understand why the learning matters in their life—educators recognize that cultural relevance is not just tied to the student's historical background (e.g., Mexican history and culture), but rather reflects the students immediate and local reality (e.g., growing up Mexican American in the local community of the school). • Educators employ positive learning environment strategies in the classroom and throughout the school that provide connection and engagement for each and every student—this includes inclusive classroom management strategies, mentors or significant adults for each student, knowing and using student names, fostering relationships with parents and guardians, and "failure is not an option" instructional methods.	heritage while also having multiple opportunities to gain proficiency in skill-based learning standards that clearly spell out for students why the learning matters, as illustrated in personalized curriculum sets that are relevant for students and drive them in an organized way toward college and career readiness performance standards. • On a day-by-day basis, students feel validated and honored within the classroom because of a powerful combination of strong student–teacher relationships, positive classroom and school environments, individual learning supports, a rigorous academic program, and high expectations—this requires that the school has clearly laid out learning goals and standards for all involved, and why they matter for each and every student.

gaps in effectiveness might exist—is the school's inclusive culture limited in its success due to *personal* doubts, *institutional* limitations, or lack of *professional* skill in building effective learning environments?

There are no perfect strategies or even true "best practices" since every educational initiative, teacher action, or school characteristic necessitates localized application so that it is responsive to the immediate learning and social needs of the actual students served. Thus, it is up to you, the educator, to identify the best practices that work with your own students so that all will find success within your classrooms.

EQUITY CHARACTERISTICS WITHIN CULTURE

Figure 2.2   The Equity Framework: Characteristics

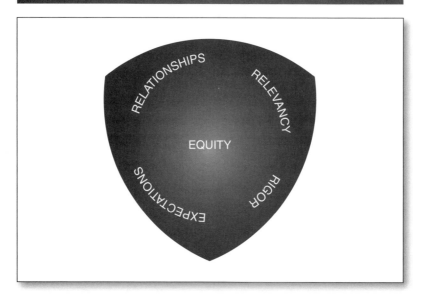

Within these equitable schools that form the basis for the equity framework, we also observed four common characteristics of equity: expectations, rigor, relevancy, and relationships. As equity characteristics, they encircle equity, symbolizing that without these four present for *all* students, no matter their diversity, other school improvement efforts may struggle to succeed. These four characteristics are key to accomplishing equity—and all define the impact a school's equitable culture will have on students.

- *Expectations* set the bar for high achievement.
- *Rigor* provides the skills and learning the student needs to succeed.

- *Relevancy* directs the teacher in providing instruction and curriculum that relates to and connects with the learner.
- *Relationships* help the student believe the teacher's high expectations, engage with the rigorous curriculum, and respond to the relevancy of the learning.

These four primary elements are found in an equitable and culturally competent school culture where the adults and the children feel socially accepted and valued. Addressing school culture focuses on creating spaces where every individual's voice is valued and respected and the collective team of staff, students, and families work together toward a common vision.

These four characteristics are key to the ongoing and successful efforts of any equity-minded school trying to build a culture of achievement and respect that works for all students, regardless of race, gender, language, ethnicity, economics, and difference from cultural and social norms. Consequently, the four characteristics of equity form the basis of the rest of this book. In the following chapters, the "how-to" of building and sustaining equitable school culture is presented through each of these characteristics.

THE EQUITY LENS

By analyzing yourself personally, institutionally, and professionally through an equity lens, you can understand where you and your school need to go to *equitize* the schooling experience for all students.

As first presented in *Equity 101: The Equity Framework,* the equity lens illustrated here uses the equity framework to guide you in examining your leadership, culture, and practice. In doing this, you will describe who you are in terms of equity (personal), measure the equity within your system (institutional), and analyze the equitable nature of your programs and practices (professional). By applying an equity lens to yourself and your institution, you will paint a clearer picture of what you and your school need to do to achieve equity.

In *Cultural Proficiency: A Manual for School Leaders,* Randall Lindsey, Kikanza Nuri Robins, and Raymond Terrell state what they believe we need to do to achieve equity: We need to become culturally proficient. Cultural proficiency, they write, is an "inside-out

Figure 2.3 The **E**quity Lens

CULTURE

Personal Strategies

- Study what it means to be White, and what it means to be of color in our society.
- Analyze my own life in terms of Whiteness and diversity.

Institutional Strategies

- Create a collaborative environment wherein all voices are valued and supported.
- Develop institutionalized safety and respect for all diversities.

Professional Strategies

- Engage in regular conversations with people different from myself in order to build understanding.
- Represent diversity in all my work.

PRACTICE

Personal Strategies

- Challenge privilege provided to me according to my race.
- Minimize the myths of dominant culture in my interactions and ambitions.

Institutional Strategies

- Incorporate standards and practices that value diversity.
- Support development of excellence in all with whom I work.

Professional Strategies

- Differentiate support based upon needs and talents of people in my organization.
- Measure impact of equity efforts as diligently as other data analysis.

EQUITY

LEADERSHIP

Personal Strategies

- Engage with mentors and allies to guide me in my work toward equity.
- Study the work and writings of educators and other leaders who have worked to build equity in education and society.

Institutional Strategies

- Lead my organization in equitizing the work environment for all employees.
- Diversify workforce and provide opportunities for growth and success.

Professional Strategies

- Align all professional efforts so that they support the building of equity in schools.
- Engage all opportunities that provide a forum to disseminate equity principles.

process of personal and organizational change," and "a matter of who we are, more than what we do" (2009, p. 20).

Throughout this series, you will read different examples of schools succeeding with *all* students at the elementary, secondary, and systemic levels. An equity lens analysis will be provided for each school success story. Within all of these schools, equity is not simply a strategy to address Adequate Yearly Progress (AYP) and student achievement concerns. Equity is not just about a student's statistical performance; rather, it is about the life and actualized potential of the child.

The equity lens guides us in examining the school, its educators, and how they impact students according to equity. Following is an equity lens analysis of Apollo Middle School, illustrated in the first chapter, which describes the strategies Apollo used to build success for all students. Throughout this series, we invite you to review these equity lens analyses, and to create your own lens in the *Equity in Action* activities that conclude each chapter. When you create your own equity lens, you are engaging in reflective practice. Robert Marzano, Tina Boogren, Tammy Heflebower, Jessica Kanold-McIntyre, and Debra Pickering (2012) write that reflective practice is "acknowledged to be a powerful tool for professional development and growth. Reflective practice facilitates the processing and integration of new knowledge and can help students and practitioners make sound decisions when confronted with unfamiliar situations" (p. 4). Building a culture of equity is a journey into unfamiliar situations, and one powerful tool to mediate these situations is through reflective practice; therefore, each chapter in this book offers you the tools for both personal and collaborative reflection.

Equitable Culture in Action: Chapter 2, The Equity Framework

Equitable Culture Example

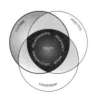

In the Equity 101 group on PD 360, watch the video featuring Apollo Middle School, titled "Changing the Weather." In the Equity 101 group, you will also find additional resources to deepen and extend your understanding of equity.

Figure 2.4 Equity Lens: Apollo Middle School

CULTURE

Personal Strategies

- Expectations and beliefs of educators challenged in regards to Apollo's student body
- "Caring" identified as most important characteristic

Institutional Strategies

- Created Community School to provide support and engagement with parents
- Created school-wide high expectations for learning

Professional Strategies

- Embraced culturally relevant teaching strategies to drive student engagement
- Facilitated strong teacher–student relationships

PRACTICE

Personal Strategies

- Lack of growth in pedagogical effectiveness unacceptable
- Teachers identify strengths and weaknesses

Institutional Strategies

- Professional development provided that models strategies across the school
- Parents educated how to support their child's academic engagement and success

Professional Strategies

- Technique provided for differentiating the instruction
- Culturally relevant curriculum and strategies implemented

EQUITY

LEADERSHIP

Personal Strategies

- Educators challenged to re-examine assumptions about achievement potential of Apollo students
- Teachers supported if they engage in change effort, and held accountable if resistant

Institutional Strategies

- Established BHAG—Big Hairy Audacious Goal—with goal of reaching high achieving status in four year's time
- Examined every aspect of school's operation

Professional Strategies

- Professional development provided based on specific teacher needs
- Embraced culturally relevant methods as primary teaching methodology

Equity Discussion

As a group, discuss the characteristics of equity through the lens of equitable school culture:

Expectations: Do the administration and the staff at your school hold high expectations for each and every student? Do the teachers at your school take as much responsibility for when their students fail as well as when they succeed? Do the students believe the teachers believe they can achieve at high levels?

Rigor: Do your students have access to a rigorous curriculum, strong teachers, and a school climate that fosters achievement? In what ways does a culture of excellence exist or not exist at your school in academic, extracurricular, and social programs?

Relevancy: How aligned is the culture and instruction of the school with the background, characteristics, and interests of the students? How do the relationships within the school reflect the values, cultures, assumptions, and beliefs of students and their community? In what culturally relevant ways does the school engage all students, socially and intellectually?

Relationships: In what ways does your school build collaborative relationships with staff, students, and the community? How does the school support students and educators alike in feeling safe to take risks and stay motivated to succeed?

Equity Lens: Professional

Describe the professional challenges that exist that limit the change of the culture in your school.

_____

_____

EQUITY ACTION #1

Which challenge might you address first? What actions might you take?

_____

_____

In the following chapters, we examine more closely the characteristics of equity, using examples from real educators working in real schools. Chapter 3 focuses on expectations.

CHAPTER 3

Equitable Culture

Expectations

I n Chapter 1, you learned about Apollo Middle School's principal Ray Chavez, who holds an attitude of high expectations for his staff, his students, and himself. Determined to succeed, he led his staff and students to improved academic achievement by changing the culture of the school from one where students did not want to identify as Apollo Middle School students to one where they are proud to say they are. Principal Chavez ushered in a culture of high expectations, and he did it by changing teacher and student attitudes and belief systems. Not an easy thing to do, but with a vision of high expectations—and lots of hard work—Principal Chavez and Apollo's educators made it happen.

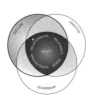

The foundations of an equitable school culture are the *expectations* that exist for its students and, by extension, the educators who serve those students. Why does a school exist? To prepare students for college or career readiness after their K–12 experience. Thus, everything that happens in a school should flow from this expectation. Anything that is less expected than this educational goal guarantees that not all students will gain the skills and knowledge they need to succeed in life after school.

To build equity, schools need to address the expectations of administrators and teachers alike. In particular, what are the true expectations that the individual professionals in the school hold for students? Furthermore, do the educators take responsibility for their students' success and failure? Without this culture of responsibility tied to defined expectations, teachers will continue blaming students and their background for low performance rather than claiming ownership of student learning.

We describe equitable culture as consisting of both a positive learning environment and cultural competency on the part of the educators. Foundationally, the equity characteristic of expectations defines both of these components:

1. Effective and safe learning culture is deliberately fostered for students and educators alike to support the growth that must happen for each individual student to achieve the high expectations set by the school, the students, the parents, and the community.

2. Cultural competence empowers every teacher and administrator to honestly surface and address biases, doubts, and differences that may exist so as to remove these barriers and actualize high expectations for each and every student, regardless of who the student is or where he or she comes from.

After reflecting on these components of effective equitable school culture, think about how you participate in your own school's culture. Your participation is expressed most importantly through your attitudes and expectations for students, colleagues, and yourself. Your attitudes form your perceived reality, and thus influence your honest expectations. Teachers and students can be caught in a perceived reality that keeps each individual from attaining his or her potential (Lindsey, Roberts, & Campbell Jones, 2005), so it is imperative that we examine perceived school culture in comparison with actual institutional characteristics. Eliminating low achievement requires educators to honestly reexamine the cultural expectations that exist within their schools to identify all inherent weaknesses.

Unfortunately, schools tend to spend little time identifying cultural characteristics that both engage and disengage educators and students, thus leaving many educators unskilled in improving school cultures. To illustrate this point, identify two separate institutions: one that you enjoy where you feel safe and actively engaged, and another that you like less where you may disengage and feel uncomfortable. Either of these could be a church, club, athletic group or event, cultural institution, or even your own family's home. In Worksheet 3.1, list the institutions and describe several characteristics of these institutions that make you feel engaged or disengaged.

Compare and contrast your school's culture to the engaging and disengaging institutions you described earlier. What is similar? What is different? In what institution do you have higher expectations for yourself and others in that institution? Would you define your school's culture as more like the engaging or the disengaging institution? Share your reflection with colleagues and in the online Equity 101 community.

Worksheet 3.1 Comparing and Contrasting Engagement

Engaging Institution: Disengaging Institution:

Institutional Characteristics: Institutional Characteristics:

You may describe the characteristics of the engaging institution as freedom of expression, time for solitude, and individual responsibility. Or you may have listed communal decision making, social interaction, and collective responsibility. The characteristics you listed reflect the values you honor and support, and these are the areas within which you have the greatest voice when advocating for institutional improvement. For your school to achieve success with all students, your voice needs to be "in the air" in support of an equitable culture that represents the needs of all stakeholders. How does your school culture honor and value the voice of each adult and each child?

High Expectations: Belief Systems

Adults who work in a school are not very different from the students who attend the school. We all look for an environment—a *culture*—where we feel validated for who we are and that reinforces our belief systems. Educational culture stems from the institutional belief system that characterizes a school. The roots of educational failure and of academic success both are found within the cultural characteristics embodied by the educators of the school. It is the adults in the school building who foster and reinforce the school's culture, no matter what that culture may be.

Thus, if our belief systems are based on the Bell Curve, and we believe only a percentage of students have the ability to succeed, then we are validated rather than upset by a certain percentage of failures in our classes. For example, more than 30% of students in many high schools are failing freshman and sophomore math, yet the educators in these schools do not always take public responsibility for these failures. Operating under the paradigm that some students have the ability to learn high school math and others don't ensures student failure.

During a recent professional development workshop that Bonnie conducted on research-based strategies, a math teacher asked for strategies to introduce more rigor into the classroom. Bonnie asked how the educator would know that using the more rigorous instruction was a success. The teacher answered, "Because more students will fail." If students know they have a high probability of failing a class, it is hard for them to respond to encouragement to try harder.

As adults, how often do we voluntarily engage in experiences where we are prone to fail? And when we do, how do we feel? Rather than motivating us, the added stress and threat of imminent failure typically causes us to shut down, and students are no different.

A successful school culture exhibits a symbiotic relationship between students who *want* to be there and educators who *enjoy* working there. If we want to succeed, then we naturally want to be where we are safe to take risks and motivated to succeed. The challenge lies in taking responsibility for creating this type of school culture—responsibility that is inherently thrust upon the professionals within the schoolhouse.

At Rancho Verde High School in California, students clearly understand the high expectations teachers have of them. The school uses the national AVID program, which stands for *Advancement Via Individual Determination.* AVID is a program that teaches college-prep skills to students who may not otherwise have considered college, and illuminates the potential within these students for all teachers to see. When principal Michael McCormick identified potential students for the program, he met with them personally and let them know that the school expects them to succeed in AVID, and how it will lead to opportunities such as college. "I really think it is about expectations," he said. Rancho Verde AVID coordinator Vivien Kearney shared, "Our [AVID students] are more ready than even some of [the schools] brightest because they have the tools." Because of AVID, more students take AP classes, and 98% of AVID students attend college. Rancho Verde's institutional belief system guides this culture of high expectations for all students.

Preventing student failure is also illustrated by Becky Clark, a second-grade teacher in Perris, California who teaches entirely English-language learners. She knows that most of her new students will not be speaking any English, yet she must teach them to speak and read English by the end of second grade. This is not merely a "hope" she holds since her practice in the classroom legitimizes the expectations. She uses the method of "Say it, see it, read it, write it." Skills, concepts, and standards are posted; she checks them off regularly and uses them for instruction. Attitudinally, this is a teacher who has reflected on her strengths and weaknesses, is aware of what she must do, and sincerely expects all of her students to achieve.

These educators model the importance of a belief system that holds high expectations for all students. Teachers who model this approach modify their instruction and classroom environments to suit student needs. Furthermore, they intently listen to the insights students offer into what high expectations and a culture of trust look like in the classroom.

When asked what they wanted from their teachers, eighth-grade students at a middle school in Maryland shared the following:

- Make learning fun
- Allow student discussions about the topic
- Don't use lecture all the time
- Care about the students by asking them about their lives
- Teach "hard stuff" and let students know that teachers expect them to learn it
- Help them when they need help with the lessons
- Build physical movement into the lessons so that students do not have to sit the entire period
- Teach using a project-oriented curriculum
- Do not use sarcasm or a ridiculing tone of voice

These students know exactly what they want from their teachers—a school culture that embraces engagement and high expectations.

High Expectations: Culturally Proficient Communication Styles

Expectations set the bar for high achievement. One way we relay our expectations is through our communication. Communication styles vary from culture to culture and may be misread by a teacher unfamiliar with the culture of his or her students. When teachers are unaware of the nonverbal cues of their students, they may assume the student is being disrespectful when he or she is not. Think about a time when you thought a student was being disrespectful, but you were not completely convinced. What was the student saying? Doing? Physically showing in face and body? It is possible that what you read were the nonverbal communication styles naturally expressed by the child. If unaware of how to read nonverbal cues, this can appear as defiance or a disconnect in student communication.

Once, in a classroom, Curtis observed a White teacher trying to personally connect with a Latino American student. Through his nonverbal actions, the boy was showing that he felt like he did not fit in this classroom—choosing to sit alone at a table in the back, not participating in the class discussion, not looking up at the teacher, and buried under the hood of his sweatshirt. In an attempt to connect verbally with the student, the teacher informed him that she had visited Mexico the previous summer, without ever asking the student if he was of Mexican descent or had ever even been to Mexico. The teacher told the student that she had met people in Mexico with his same last name, but they pronounced the name with a Spanish accent, whereas the student pronounced his last name with an English accent. Nonverbally through physical expression, the student recoiled at this suggestion that the teacher had discovered a more "proper" way for this student to pronounce his own last name. Unintentionally, the teacher verbally communicated to the student that she might know more about his heritage and background than even he did—and the student responded nonverbally by disengaging, looking down, and not responding to the teacher.

Dealing with differences can be intimidating. As educators, we need to study and learn about the history, culture, and values of our diverse students. We also want our students to learn about each other. Teachers at North Glendale Elementary School in Kirkwood, MO, have their students do self-portraits on a poster and answer the question, "Who am I?" Students' portraits are displayed throughout the year in the classrooms. Students have an opportunity to view and discuss their perceptions of themselves and others. This exercise provides the opportunity for teachers and students to talk in an "unpacked, uncharged way." In the online Equity 101 community, describe an activity you use in your classroom or school that helps diverse students learn about each other.

Alfred Tatum, in his book *Teaching Reading to Black Adolescent Males: Closing the Achievement Gap* (2005), helps us understand that we cannot group all Black adolescent males—and other student identities—into monolithic groups and expect to understand them. "Black males living amid turmoil may be different culturally from black males who live free of turmoil," Tatum asserts (2005, p. 72). As the son of a White mother and African American father, Bonnie's son was raised middle class, identifies as Black, and received opportunities not available to "Black males living amid turmoil." Even though others "see" him as Black, he cannot be expected to behave as a stereotypical idea of what Blackness stands for in our culture. This is one of many reasons why Bonnie lists her first principle of interacting with others as "[e]ach person is a unique individual and capable of achieving at high levels."

In the classroom, students bring with them expectations for classroom communication, and it may differ from your expectations. Students differ in the amount of classroom control they believe a teacher should exert. Students differ in their expectations for answering questions and the amount of teacher guidance they expect (Cloud, quoted in Artiles & Ortiz, 2002). Students differ in their responses to the information exposed in the classroom. The more alike the student is to the teacher, the more likely they are to share similar values and expectations. Culturally competent teachers explicitly teach their students what the expectations are in the class-room. If educators do not make these expectations for behavior and learning perfectly clear and explicit, students who differ from the teacher are placed at a disadvantage since they may not know the "hidden rules" of the classroom.

HIGH EXPECTATIONS: EDUCATOR RESPONSIBILITY

How would you define professional responsibility for an educator? Educator Jamie Almanzan states, "If a kid fails in your class, you failed. We've got to start believing that the teacher has something to do with it." The failure of a student should be a warning light to the teacher: Why did the student fail? What expectations were not present? What needs of the student were not understood?

Teaching is a challenging profession that can seem never-ending in its demands. But students rely on the professionals within the building to deliver an adequate and equitable education. The tendency to compare teaching to parenting is accurate simply because children are wholly dependent on the efforts of their parents to sustain them just as students are wholly dependent on the efforts of their teachers for their classroom education. Few educators entered teaching because of the fame, prestige, and financial rewards associated with other careers. Most became teachers because they truly care about children.

The challenge, however, is that faced with the relentless demands of today's schools, many teachers have lost the passionate flame they began with. This burnout is detrimental not only to the teacher, but especially to the student. Along with this comes a slacking of professional responsibility toward the students. To reignite this passion, teachers need to know that the effort they put forth will pay dividends in student achievement. As an equitable culture becomes more and more apparent within the classroom, educators will begin to enjoy the challenge and the successes once again. This leads to an increase in passion, which in turn deepens an educator's responsibility toward his or her students.

At Elmont Memorial High School, department chair Alicia Calabrese has seen this passion and responsibility grow within the educators she works with:

> Our faculty are just very passionate and dedicated people. They are very committed to each and every child in their care. They get very involved in making each child succeed in whatever it is that they are getting them to do.

This has led to the phenomenal success of nearly a 100% graduation rate at Elmont Memorial.

The students at Elmont likewise notice this passion, dedication, and educator responsibility. Senior Tasha Brown commented,

> They all love what they do, they have a passion for what they teach. So when they're teaching us, their love for what they do comes across. You have to love what you do before you try to teach it to somebody else.

Effective school culture relies on strong and passionate professional attitudes of high expectations coupled with a deeply held responsibility for student success on the part of the educators. Our students will succeed as long as we are responsible for the high expectations we hold for them.

To measure your expectations toward students, analyze your reactions to students not only when they succeed but also when they fail. Regardless of what we verbalize to students, if we are shocked when they succeed, we need to examine why, and if we are not shocked when they fail, we have even more relevant data for self-examination. When you use the data of failure to inform how you modify your instruction and reteach what has not yet been learned, you are holding high expectations for students and actively supporting their success.

Typically, when educators talk about the need for high expectations, they are referencing what they expect students to achieve. While we support this, there is another dimension of high expectations found within equitable schools: what educators expect of themselves. Traditionally, there has been a forced equanimity among educators where culturally teachers are not supposed to "boast" publicly about their talents and accomplishments. Think of the "Teacher of the Year" recipient whose acceptance speech is all about how "we are *all* good teachers," and consequently shares none of his or her skills with the rest of the staff. And yet, the reality is that these teachers are highly skilled and talented, and their knowledge needs to be disseminated.

The most successful educators take pride in themselves as powerful teachers who do not expect their students to fail and do everything necessary to support their success. This attitude of high expectation is grounded within the best professionalism. As one trained to teach, educators exhibit respect to the teaching profession by expecting the most of students because they expect the most from their own efforts. As a teacher communicates these high expectations in the classroom, students come to believe in the talent of the teacher, which means they can't fail this class. The teacher communicates "I am *too good* for you to fail." When this happens in a school, the Bell Curve becomes irrelevant because students strive toward high achievement, rather than persisting in mediocrity.

As teachers share their strengths with students, they also need to be honest about their weaknesses. If a teacher is a great writing coach, let the students know that they can trust this teacher to help them write well. And if the teacher is not strong in another area, do not mislead the child, but point him or her in the right direction to another educator who can help the student. Students greatly respect this honesty. As they learn to trust that the teacher will always be honest with them, then the student finds it easier to believe and reach the high expectations expressed to them by the teacher. What expectations do you hold for yourself as an educator?

THE ATTITUDE OF HIGH EXPECTATIONS

Merissa, a student at Apollo Middle School, sums up the benefit of a shift in school culture when she says,

Some kid would come up to me and say, "What middle school do you go to?" I say, "I go to Apollo." He said, "Oh, I feel bad for you." But now they say, "Well that's good, I heard it's a very good school."

Educator and student expectations cohesively meet when the school offers a rigorous academic environment coupled with high expectations, and the trust that students can achieve. In this type of a school, students believe they can succeed because they know their teachers will not allow it to be any other way.

EQUITABLE CULTURE IN ACTION: CHAPTER 3, EXPECTATIONS

Equitable Culture: Expectations Example

In the Equity 101 group on PD 360, watch the video segment titled "Changing the Mindset" from the program *Equity and Innovation: Apollo Middle School.* This video segment describes how Apollo Middle School created a culture of high expectations. In the Equity 101 group, you will also find additional resources to deepen and extend your understanding of equity.

Equity Discussion

Online conversations: Describe the culture of expectations at your school.

Expectations: Do the administration and the staff hold high expectations for each student at your school? Do the teachers at your school take as much responsibility for when their students fail as well as when they succeed? Do the students believe the teachers believe they can achieve at high levels?

How does the culture of expectations at your school foster or not foster student achievement?

What works, what doesn't, and what is being done to develop a culture of high expectations?

_____

_____

Equity Lens: Professional

What challenge might you address to improve the culture of expectations at your school?

_____

_____

EQUITY ACTION #1

What actions might you take to address low expectations in your classrooms and throughout the school?

_____

_____

This chapter examined high expectations and what they look like in a school setting. In the next chapter, you will examine the meaning of rigor and what rigor looks like in real schools.

CHAPTER 4

Equitable Culture

Rigor

*R*igor provides the skills and learning the student needs to succeed.

Rigor is not about difficulty of the curriculum, nor is rigor about the toughness of the educator. In an equitable school, rigor places the learning within stretchable reach of each and every student—a rigorous learning culture optimizes student engagement so that individual students learn what they personally need to progress and accelerate academically. In traditional equity discussions, rigor is addressed abstractly as necessary for the achievement of students of color and other marginalized students. In courageous conversations about equity, rigor expands to include "refocusing schooling on the children's educational needs rather than on the personal needs of the adults who inhabit the buildings" (Singleton & Linton, 2006, p. 228). When schools focus on *children's* educational needs rather than on *adults'* needs, student success climbs. Progress occurs where energy is placed: If a school spends its emotional energy on managing adult relations, student learning suffers; if a school *rigorously* focuses its energies on the individualized educational needs of students, achievement soars. Even though we profess to be all about students, many of our actions say otherwise. This is why rigor is needed within equitable school culture.

One of the most rigorous learning environments Curtis and his video production crew at the School Improvement Network ever documented was at a truly open and free high school campus. An entirely self-directed and freewheeling campus seems contradictory with high-achieving academic rigor, but this is the reality at the West Hawaii Explorations Academy (WHEA) on the Kona Coast of the Big Island of Hawaii. South of the airport in the lava fields above the crashing waves of the ocean lies an open-air campus spread across several acres. There are no permanent buildings or classrooms. But there are dozens of rigorous science experiments being conducted by students across the campus:

- An aquaponics experiment where students are comparing the growth rates of plants based on the organic and chemical fertilizers placed in the water

- A student-built robot that can pick up a basketball and dunk it in the basket

- An octopus tank where students are training the octopus to open bottles and navigate a maze

- A rainmaker system where cold water pumped up from deep in the ocean is pushed through coiled pipes, causing condensation of moisture from the air, and collected to irrigate the dozens of student agriculture projects

- A shark tank constructed by a special education student where an injured black-tip reef shark has been successfully rehabilitated

Amazed at the dozens of student-led projects currently being conducted, Curtis sat down with the students to discuss how these fascinating research projects translated into academic rigor. Two students sat down in front of him, pulled out a thick binder, and walked him through their report. At more than 80 pages in length, similar reports are required of all students multiple times per year. Page after page revealed analytical charts, reviews of the academic literature and research on the topic, annotated lists of resources and references, interviews with local experts and researchers, and analysis from peer-review groups. This was academic work that surpassed most college rigor, but was a normal part of the students' day-to-day engagement.

With very little funding, informal organization, and no real buildings, the staff at WHEA has built the most rigorous high school program in the islands of Hawaii. Year after year, WHEA students have the highest writing and literacy scores of all high school students in Hawaii—this despite the fact that there is no actual English or writing classes. Rigor is inherent within the learning, rather than a conscious "add-on" to traditional curriculum. Students choose and direct their own research projects, but teachers and community mentors drive them to rigorously conduct the experiments and achieve excellence in their academic reporting. This is a campus where almost every student who enters graduates prepared for college, career, and beyond. Rigor defines WHEA, rather than WHEA trying to determine how to apply it.

RIGOR WITHIN EQUITY

Within an equitable school culture, rigor defines excellence. Recall the definition of educational equity: *Educators provide all students with the individual support they need to reach and exceed a common standard.* Within this definition, equity calls for all students to "reach and exceed a common standard." But without clearly identifying this standard—and assuring that it is rigorous—equity becomes only a mind-set, not a reality. Culturally equitable schools establish effective standards that define college and career readiness for every student, and then create strong learning goals for each individual student towards those standards.

In the United States, the Common Core State Standards initiative provides a rigorous framework that defines college and career readiness performance standards. If a school's equitable culture focuses its efforts on the lifelong effect of a student's education, college and career readiness becomes a reasonable goal. No school improvement effort can guarantee lifelong success for every student, but educational systems *can* guarantee that each student has the necessary skill sets and proficiency levels to succeed at college or advanced career training and application.

An equitable school first prepares students for success and then sends the student off into the world ready to work hard and succeed individually, educationally, socially, financially, and emotionally. The goal is that students can go out and succeed on their own. But this most likely happens if they are prepared for college and career on leaving high school. The Common Core standards are skill and competency based rather than primarily knowledge based, like most previous state standards. Thus, they work well to establish rigor and to set attainable goals for students. When students clearly understand the skill they must master, they can pursue it rigorously. When learning targets are vague, students and teachers alike aim toward amorphous goals.

When an equitable school engages the Common Core Standards, these learning goals get focused and aimed at the individual learning styles and needs of each student. Within this tailoring of a rigorous and individualized learning experience, teachers develop a broad understanding of the cultural backgrounds and learning characteristics of their students, thus providing rigor and relevance in education.

DEFINING RIGOROUS CULTURE

In *The Learning Leader* (2006), Douglas Reeves suggests asking groups of educators the following question: "What causes student achievement?" He suggests that the conversation will take one of two different turns: Either staff will focus on the adults and say things such as "curriculum, feedback, assessment, expectations, multidisciplinary lessons, engaging lessons, multiple opportunity for success, and writing and reading across the curriculum," or the responses will be about the kids and will include things such as "poverty level of students, ethnicity of student, home language of students, and parent monitoring of schoolwork" (2006, p. 75). The "curious" finding of the research states that

> if you believe that adults make a difference in student achievement, you are right. If you believe that adults are helpless bystanders while demographic characteristics work their inexorable will on the academic lives of students, you are right. Both of these statements become self-fulfilling prophesies. (2006, p. 76)

Equitable excellence also becomes a self-fulfilling prophecy when school culture focuses on building rigor in student and teacher development. When looking at rigor through the two lenses of equitable culture—a learning culture and cultural competency—it is evident the role that rigor plays in achieving a school environment where educators and students alike are supported in their drive to success:

- Rigor in an effective and safe learning culture defines the skills and learning the student needs to succeed, and organizes learning at a level that appropriately stretches the student.
- On a daily basis, culturally competent educators apply culturally relevant learning strategies so that students can spend their efforts on rigorously developing necessary skills and proficiencies, rather than having to find ways to connect with the learning.

A rigorous school culture focuses first on students. Rigor provides the skills and learning the student needs to succeed, and in such a culture, students are explicitly taught and continually inundated with aural and visual messages telling them they are part of a successful, rigorous culture.

To illustrate rigor within an equitable school culture, consider two high schools: During the morning announcements of School A, students hear about the football team, the dance on Friday night, the car wash on Saturday, and maybe the Honor Society. In School B, although they do not exclude this information, it is balanced and even weighted more heavily toward academic announcements:

- "Mr. Jackson from the local university will meet with students in Room 201 today"
- "Jennie Davies won first place in the Monsanto Math Competition for the state"
- "The following students are National Merit Finalists . . ."
- "Today's tutoring session will focus on the following subjects . . ."

School B emphasizes the academic rigor of the school mission as it applies to the success of all students by continually building a culture of rigor, while School A continues to place emphasis only on those students seen as traditionally exceptional, thus maintaining the status quo that only some students will succeed within a culture of mediocre academic rigor.

Rigor means we strongly focus on students' academic needs. Barbara Bredemeier, reading teacher at Richardson High School, in

Richardson, Texas, says that their dropout rate is less than 1% because they focus first on students. Barry Brooks, counselor at Amherst Middle School, in Amherst, Massachusetts, says that their teachers reach out to individual students, invite them to come for extra help and clarification on content, and sincerely care for each one of them. The equitable culture of the school lets students know they are the most important focus within the school.

To analyze your own school's culture of rigor, first make a list of the programs and initiatives you do in your school to demonstrate that you clearly focus on students and set the tone for academic rigor. Next, make a list of the programs and initiatives you do in your school that do not directly impact academic rigor. Which list is longer? Which list gets more energy and attention from the administration? From teachers? From students? From the community? Is your school one where academic rigor is the primary focus or not?

When we focus first and foremost on the learning needs of students, we usually find all students achieving. Yet, in some schools, we still find special education students relegated to the back room of the bottom floor, AP classes filled only with White and Asian students, and academic groups such as the National Honor Society homogenous and unrepresentative of the school's diverse demographics. Are any of these homogenous groups in your school? Which ones? Why do you think they remain homogenous?

STUDENT POTENTIAL AS DEFINED BY RIGOR

Think about the culture of rigor in your school. What tells you there is rigor?

Some educators do not have a clear picture of what rigor looks like, and Bonnie confesses she was one. She taught for more than 20 years in a district that emphasized its sporting teams but not its academic teams. With a reputation of being a sound district, its students scored just above the mean on state tests, and most teachers thought they were doing a good job of instruction. Most of the students in this district were from blue-collar backgrounds, and often would be the first generation in their family to attend college. Without a school culture that clearly understood academic rigor, teachers often managed classrooms where boys ridiculed girls in advanced classes for demonstrating their intelligence, and not all students were seen as having the potential for high levels of learning.

Bonnie often found herself having to explicitly discuss these actions with her senior class, insisting there could be no "eye-rolling," smirks, or negative comments in the class. At the same time, she had to tell her students, especially the girls, that they were not allowed to begin their responses or readings with any negative comment, such as "It's not very good, but . . ." In fact, not cutting oneself down before sharing a response became one of the norms Bonnie established in the 12th-grade advanced writing class.

When Bonnie moved from this district to a highly achieving district well known for its academic achievement and college attendance rate, she discovered that the rigor of learning in her former school was a couple of years behind what students did in her new school. Even the freshman and sophomore literature chosen for students to read in her new school was what middle school students were reading in the former school. Clearly, the students in the new district experienced a more rigorous curriculum, were better prepared for career and college, and statistically showed that they were succeeding after high school graduation at much higher rates.

Part of an equitable school culture includes modeling for students what rigor looks like—both during school and after their K–12 experience:

- In Chapel Hill, North Carolina, teachers turn their classrooms into mini-universities. They each choose a university, post banners from the school, and fill their rooms with artifacts from that university and their own college experience. Teachers plot out their journey to and through the university, complete with photos. In their instruction, they say things such as "When you are at University of North Carolina, this is what you will be expected to know." They post the year the students will graduate from college, and their hallways are named after universities. Throughout the school, the culture of rigor tells these students that they will be successful and will attend a university of their choice.
- At North Glendale Elementary in St. Louis County, Missouri, students write their goals and the steps they will take to reach the goals, and then post them in the hallways for all to see. As

students walk by, they continually see the plan they have mapped out for themselves.

- In Detroit, Michigan, students who are part of the Michigan Education Achievement Authority engage in a standards-centered approach where students individually pursue proficiency in the College and Career Readiness Standards, rather than simply spending time in grade levels. This allows students to constantly be engaged in rigorous learning based on each student's individual needs and readiness levels.

Students are unquestionably affected by the culture of rigor in their schools. One educator Bonnie worked with shared that she came from a family living in poverty where no one went to college. When she was an adolescent, however, her father moved them to a school district where nearly everyone attended college. Because her peers were all going to attend college, she assumed she would too, and she did. As educators and as students, we are affected by the learning culture that surrounds us. This is why creating a culture of rigor in the school—not just making learning rigorous—supports the academic success of all students, no matter who they are or where they come from.

CREATING A CULTURE OF RIGOR

Rigor is not an abstract concept. Nor is it just making learning hard for students. Rigor is a characteristic of equitable schools that can be developed, nurtured, and sustained in any school culture. Teachers can engage multiple strategies that build an equitable culture:

- Post pictures of role models in academic areas throughout the school.
- Invite former successful students to talk with classes.
- Use "college talk" in instruction.
- Have students set goals and write out the steps to achieving those goals.
- Post learning goals and standards throughout the school.
- Illustrate for students the lifelong benefits of achieving proficiency within the various standards.

- Designate one high school counselor to be the "college counselor" and work with students on applying to and getting into college.
- Hold academic honor assemblies.
- Include academic contests and honors in the morning announcements.
- Celebrate small steps by all students.

Rigor provides the skills and learning the student needs to succeed. Students of any age are remarkably aware of what teachers do to help them succeed. According to the students at J. Erik Jonsson Elementary School—an inner-city school of mainly poor Latino students in Dallas, Texas—their teachers do the following culturally competent things to drive a rigorous learning experience:

Eli Gonzalez: Whenever we'll do like one subject, teachers keep on trying to teach it in multiple ways 'cause if kids don't get it one way there is always other ways to do it.

Melody Gomez: They also use centers that are like games. They put us into little small groups. While she has a small group at the back table that she's teaching, we go around the room with partners to little games, and those games help us learn more about what she was trying to teach us.

Adriana Banda: Another thing, the teachers show you strategies for you to feel more confident in yourself.

Melody Gomez: Teachers also say that if we have any strategies we can tell them, so we can also help the class.

Martin Valdez: And we have after school programs. The people that need more in help in math, science, or reading can stay after school. They can pick you to help you more so you can get commended. They help us a lot. They want everybody to get commended 'cause they believe in us.

Asked the question whether or not they think they will each attend college, these students enthusiastically responded, "Yes!" The students were then asked what the school does to help them realize this goal:

Adriana Banda: The teachers, 'cause you can always do it, and you don't need to give up. And so, even though when you're doing it you don't understand the concept, you still keep trying to get a good understanding of it.

Eli Gonzalez: Yeah, and if the teachers see you're about to give up, they won't let you give up because you'll end up having to try, and it will eventually pay off.

Melody Gomez: They believe in us. And they show to us that it is very important to keep on trying.

This interview illustrates from the students' point of view how teachers can build an equitable culture and meet the needs of diverse students. This is in a school where most of the teachers and administration are White, but most of the students are of color, come from a background of poverty, and are English-language learners. But the success of the approach speaks for itself: More than two-thirds of the students when they leave J. Eric Jonsson enter middle school over 18 months ahead of sixth-grade-level performance. Cultural proficiency can be learned and applied in rigorous ways, and these educators are living proof of its positive impact on student performance. As the teachers monitor and adjust to meet their diverse students' needs, they continue their own journey of cultural awareness.

EQUITABLE CULTURE IN ACTION: CHAPTER 4, RIGOR

Equitable Culture: Rigor Example

In the Equity 101 group on PD 360, watch the video segment titled "Defining Project Based Learning" from the program *Equity and Innovation: West Hawai'i Explorations Academy.* This video segment describes how WHEA drives rigor through project-based learning. In the Equity 101 group, you will also find additional resources to deepen and extend your understanding of equity.

Equity Discussion

Rigor: Do your students have access to a rigorous curriculum, strong teachers, and a school climate that fosters achievement? In what ways does a culture of excellence exist at your school in academic, extracurricular, and social programs?

Online conversations: Discuss what you mean by rigor at your school.

How does the culture of your school foster or not foster rigorous instruction for all students?

What works, what doesn't, and what is being done to develop a culture of rigor?

Equity Lens: Professional

Describe your professional challenges to increasing rigor at your school.

_____

_____

EQUITY ACTION #1

Which challenge to increase rigor might you address first? What actions might you take?

_____

_____

In this chapter, you learned about schools that demonstrate rigor. In the next chapter, you will learn about the relevancy that needs to be evidenced in today's classrooms.

CHAPTER 5

Equitable Culture

Relevancy

I n an equitable school culture, learning reflects the students—their interests, background, heritage, ethnicity, language, community, family, and hopes and dreams. This is *relevancy.* For students to see the educational experience as relevant, learning needs to matter for students. This does not just mean that the learning is important and necessary for a student's future. Rather, the learning inherently engages the student's interest because the student sees him- or herself within the curriculum, the student guides the involvement with what is studied, and the student creates products that reflect knowledge gained and skills mastered.

To illustrate this simply, think of what you like to eat. Who chooses what you eat? What are the origins of what you like to eat—family, ethnicity, your own discoveries and exploration? When do you eat? How do you eat? In what quantities do you eat? All of these are choices that you make on a daily basis. Even when you eat something new, you are choosing this experience. Likewise, think about the lack of enjoyment of eating when what you want and like is not available. When students guide their own learning and engagement based on their personal preferences, the quality of the learning, and the degree of engagement both rise substantially. Creating a relevant learning culture is key to accomplishing equity for each and every student.

"Wow, I wish I could have had this kind of experience!"

This is a typical reaction by first-time visitors to the West Hawaii Explorations Academy (WHEA). Relevancy defines the student experience at WHEA as it connects the learner to instruction and curriculum. If students cannot see themselves culturally within the school or see how they personally fit within the learning culture of the school, they may feel alienated and ostracized.

Nowhere is this relevancy more obvious than at WHEA, where students go "out into the real world . . . and explore science, nature, hands-on activities, all that sort of good stuff," as explained by Curtis Muraoka, co-director of the school. Here students not only do real world "stuff," but they also have a say in how and what they will do. Heather Nakakura, a teacher, founder, and co-director of the school, describes it thus:

> We all felt that to get real learning, it needed to have something more than what was happening in the traditional classroom. We believed that you learn by doing and you should have some sort of control and say to make it meaningful to every individual. And it should be based on real world problems, situations so when they leave here they're ready for whatever they pursue. . . . They're really driving their curricular program. It's not from the teacher's perspective. It's not a top down program.

In the previous chapter, WHEA's rigor was analyzed and detailed in the numerous projects and research conducted by students. A primary reason that WHEA is able to accomplish such rigor is because the learning is so relevant to students. With each engagement in the learning, students have personally

- identified the subject based on their own interest;
- developed a research project;
- connected with a community mentor of their own choosing;
- outlined a plan of action based on their own objectives and pacing;
- determined areas of research and investigation based on their personal learning needs;
- organized a team of peers to collaborate with throughout the research; and
- personally identified learning objectives, research outcomes, and quality controls based on their own needs, expectations, and interests.

These student-lead research projects at WHEA are fundamentally relevant to individual students since each student sets every parameter of learning and engagement throughout the entire project. And yet, the research projects by design are fundamentally rigorous and standards based. Students at WHEA don't question the relevancy of what they do; they create it. What could be more relevant than 100% personal choice in learning?

RELEVANT SCHOOL CULTURE

In describing relevance within an equitable school culture, it is necessary to explore it in terms of both the learning environment and the cultural competency of the educators in guiding student learning. An equitable school culture exhibits relevancy by providing

- an effective and safe learning culture that delivers instruction which inherently connects with the students' prior knowledge and background, while also explicitly showing how the learning matters personally to the student; and
- culturally competent educators who inherently design and deliver daily instruction that matters to the student, connects with who they are, and reflects where they come from locally and culturally

In a learning environment where relevancy is a primary element, schools become a safe place for students, teachers, and families because these different stakeholders "fit." They see how they individually belong and how they are each honored in all the school represents. This relevancy creates safety for students to learn and motivates families to be involved within the school community.

Safety within a school is only partially about physical security for students and teachers. It is primarily about an environment that honors who students are, respects what they bring into the classroom, and provides them with the support they need to take risks and push the boundaries of their learning. Motivation corresponds directly with safety. Once teachers and students and families feel safe, they will be more motivated to expand their skills and try new ideas.

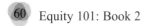

INCLUSIVE ENVIRONMENT

If students see relevancy in the learning, they feel included in the school environment. An inclusive environment is one where all students succeed at high levels within an equitable school culture. Beverly Daniel Tatum says that "it's hard to feel intellectually engaged if you're socially alienated" (Video Journal of Education, 2006). Inclusive learning environments go far beyond just being greeted and treated nicely—students see reflections of themselves, their interests, and their background in the school environment. Inclusiveness requires that the school reflect students culturally and academically.

Think back to your own educational experience. Do you see images of yourself in your educational setting? If so, what kinds of images do you see? If not, what images surrounded you? Now compare whether you remember school being a place that engaged or disengaged you. How does this correlate with the images you remember seeing in school?

Inclusiveness goes beyond learning interest to include the racial, social, ideological, cultural, linguistic, and gender backgrounds of the students. When walking into a school, students need to see reflections of themselves. Ideally, they will see themselves reflected in their teachers and administrators. However, if there are no educators who reflect the students, there are other ways to provide these reflections for the students. There might be images posted throughout the school, volunteers can come from different cultures and backgrounds, lessons can include role models from diverse ethnic and cultural groups, curriculum can reflect who students are, and students can take field trips to businesses, neighborhoods, campuses, and so on, where there are members of diverse cultural groups.

This is not to say that role models, lessons, and other learning engagements cannot come from different cultural origins than the students; nonetheless, all students need to see themselves projected visually, orally, and culturally in some manner within the school. Inclusive strategies include the following:

- Post pictures of students in classrooms and in the school.
- Take a class picture and post it on the classroom wall.
- Ask students to bring in their favorite pictures and post them in the room.

- Have students draw self-portraits and post them on the walls.
- Post images of students on computer screen backgrounds, monitors, newsletters, and other forms of communication.

When a group of struggling ninth graders were asked what would show that their teacher cared about them, one young male said, "My teacher would have a picture of me as her wallpaper on the computer screen." This young male was serious about wanting to see himself projected in the classroom where he was expected to learn. Inclusiveness requires conscious and continual effort. Educators, however, have the necessary power to project their students' images in their classrooms and throughout the rest of their schools.

AVOIDING DISENGAGEMENT

The antithesis to inclusivity in the school environment is disengagement. In a high-achieving school district Bonnie has worked with, resident students excel and go on to Ivy League universities and successful careers, but the population of African American students bussed in through a desegregation program do not perform nearly as well. There is an evident racial achievement gap. The resident population is mostly White, with a significant population of Jewish students who do not celebrate Christmas and who attend religious services on Saturday. The African American population is largely Christian and attend Black churches on Sunday in the inner city. One is not better than the other, but they are different cultures—racially, ethnically, religiously, and sometimes economically. The teaching population, also mostly White, are also mostly Christian. The district honors Winter Break, not Christmas Break, and no Christmas trimmings are allowed in the schools. When the Christmas holidays roll around each year, there is an obvious disconnect.

For students who are bussed in, it can become challenging to see oneself as part of the school community. The high school is highly competitive and rigorously academic. Staff often travel from room to room, so few walls are decorated with student work, posters, or art. Instead, success is determined by honors' classes, grade point averages, college acceptance, and competitive academic endeavors. Even though high achieving for most students, learning is not highly relevant for the most disengaged group of students.

Because the teachers are for the most part outstanding teachers of their content, Bonnie has observed that it is challenging to persuade them that relevancy matters. Most teachers were good students themselves; several were Teachers of the Year in former districts; and most have high success with the resident population. The premise of equity, however, is that *all* students engage and succeed within the school environment—not just those students most connected with the cultural norms of the school.

CULTURE OF RELEVANCY

Equitable school culture must support excellence and equal opportunity for each student who enters through the school door. Within this environment, relevancy connects the learner to instruction and curriculum, but that connection goes beyond just engagement with the content of learning. It also encompasses the emotional connection the students feel to their teachers, peers, and environment. If students are feeling alienated and ostracized, they will usually achieve far below their potential; therefore, it is education's challenge to find ways beyond the curriculum to connect the learner to the instruction—creating a culture of relevancy that holistically engages every student.

Consequently, connecting students with a culture of relevancy begins through an emotional connection where students feel accepted and ready to learn because they feel intuitively safe and capable of taking risks within the school environment. One way students gain this sense of security is through observing the staff and administrators treat each other with respect and honor. When students sense this atmosphere of respect, they often mirror the behavior. As students feel safe and valued, and are given relevant instructional opportunities, they tend to rise to their potential. WHEA co-director Heather Nakakura says, "You need to learn to step back and let the kids pursue their ideas, and you'd be amazed at what can be accomplished."

An effective culture of relevancy depends on the student feeling as though he or she is represented within the school, and that the school represents the student's personal needs and interests. Building this culture demands constant attention from educators to assure relevancy in all student engagement. Following are some strategies to create a culture of relevancy:

1. Create a teacher/student mentoring program.

2. Hold family and community potlucks where the student and his or her family can form relationships and emotional bonds to other school stakeholders.

3. Include a variety of ethnic, racial, gender, and socioeconomic students in extracurricular activities such as school plays, orchestra, academic clubs, athletic teams, and other activities.

4. Examine student shows, exhibits, and performances. Do they interest only certain group of students, or do they have relevancy for all kinds of students?

5. Ensure that all visuals in the school include all the cultures and ethnicities of the student population.

6. Hold professional development for teachers on cultural awareness and cultural relevance.

7. Create student homerooms or cadre groups where teachers can be responsible for a small group of students, get to know them well, and support them in feeling connected to the school.

8. Conduct student surveys to discover student areas of interest so as to inform instruction and curriculum.

9. Form student interest clubs, especially those that can appeal to students who may feel alienated, such as a writing club, skateboard team, cultural events clubs that focus on current genres, support groups for those who feel marginalized, and other specialized interest groups.

10. Engage students and teachers in classroom and school team building throughout the school year.

11. Invite students to participate in professional development.

12. Set up community service opportunities.

13. Ask staff to identify students who need extra attention and create opportunities for them to interact with adults in the building.

One of the most efficient ways to connect students to curriculum and instruction is through their families. Sharon Brittingham at Frankford Elementary required teachers to keep a family communication log and contact 10 parents a month. She also required that teachers meet each parent in person and let her know if the teacher was unsuccessful in making contact so that the principal could reach out personally to the parent. While principal at Northrich Elementary, Sandy Nobles required her teachers do home visits of each student in August before the school year begins. A key focus of all these contacts was identifying areas of student interest and student learning needs so as to inform relevancy in the classroom.

In her former high school, Bonnie was required to call the home of each student before the opening of school. Even though she was calling scores of homes, she admitted it was worth it when the student came in and said, "You called my mom. She said she talked to you." Bonnie adds that after several days of calling, she did feel relief (and a little guilt) when she got an answering machine and could leave a message and move on.

Reflect on the difference in your relationships with students when you knew one personally and could provide personalized relevancy for that student in your instruction and curriculum. In terms of student engagement, little is more powerful than a personalized culture of relevancy that pervades the academic experience of each and every student.

CULTURAL COMPETENCY

Relevancy requires you to know who your students are. But without understanding who you are, you will struggle to fully understand your students. Examine your student population. In what ways do your students differ from yourself? When we seek to build relationships across cultures and understand our students who are different from us, we can accelerate learning in diverse classrooms.

Diverse learners often

Practice different communication styles from the dominant culture . . . May need different teaching strategies from the dominant culture . . . May require a relationship with you, the teacher, before they decide to learn from you . . . And may be confronting personal issues about which you are unfamiliar. (Davis, 2006, p. 13)

In learning about other cultures, we realize that cultural groups differ from each other and hold differing values. These values are neither good nor bad, but are neutral and simply human responses to life that may differ between groups. A problem can arise, however, if we privilege one group's norms and values (especially our own) over another's, or simply neglect to give respect to other students' cultures and values.

In the list that follows, define your own cultural and ethnic background in comparison to your various students.

Define your own	Define your students'
Race:	Races:
Gender:	Genders:
Ethnicity:	Ethnicities:
Language:	Languages:
Economics:	Economics:
Ideologies:	Ideologies:
Interests:	Interests:
Strengths:	Strengths:
Weaknesses:	Weaknesses:

After comparing yourself with your students, what are the cultural and learning similarities and differences between you, the teachers you work with, and your students? What are the challenges you face in designing instruction and curriculum that is relevant to your student population? How successful have you been in creating a culturally relevant learning environment?

Cultural competency is the skill set necessary to connect with, understand, and support students, families, communities, and colleagues who differ from you. The equity framework is designed to guide your journey toward success with all students. As you think of your own cultural competency, reflect on your skill levels and discuss with colleagues suggestions for improving the cultural competency of the entire staff in your school. As a staff, consider engaging in the following activities:

- Take part in a series of book studies focused on cultural competency.
- Choose a culture to study for the year.
- Invite families and community leaders from other cultures into the school to share their insight and expertise.
- Create relaxed, social situations for families from different cultures to interact, meet others, and spend time with your school's staff.
- Write out your journey to cultural competency and share with colleagues.
- Become a journal buddy with a student or colleague from another cultural background.
- Attend cultural events that differ from your own.
- Ask your students to share their cultures with you both formally and informally, and teach you and your students things about their culture.
- Highlight cultural traditions, artifacts, music, and art from different cultures.
- Remain open to learning "what you don't know you don't know."

RESPETO

Gary Howard, author of *We Can't Teach What We Don't Know* (1999), suggests we show our students *respeto*—a Spanish word that goes beyond respect. It means that I, as an individual, will deeply honor you both as a person and as someone different from myself. It is often translated to mean "deference" and "esteem" in addition to simply respect. In practice, *respeto* guides me to decide that simply because I respect you, I will change who I am to become connected with you—despite our differences.

Instead of traditionally expecting students to adjust to the teacher, as teachers change their own actions and expectations in response to their students, they overcome differences between themselves and the students. This ensures that teachers more successfully lead all students to achieve because they personally guide the respectful relationships with their students. With *respeto*, educators truly engage the equity framework, holding high expectations, implementing rigor, creating relevancy, and building powerful relationships.

The following strategies help educators learn about and develop *respeto* for other cultures in their own lives:

- Attend art events given by or about people of other cultures.
- Become friends with people of other cultures.
- Have honest discussions with people of other cultures where you listen intently to their stories and beliefs.
- Live in integrated neighborhoods.
- Consider the implications of policies and politics on people of different cultures.
- Read the literature of other cultures.
- Travel to other countries.
- Place value on students' home languages and cultures.
- Study a foreign language.

In the classroom, the following strategies can help you and your students develop *respeto* for other cultures, particularly the cultures of differing students:

- Talk about the important contributions of cultural groups.
- Bring in positive articles about people of different cultures to share with students.
- Post simple phrases in multiple languages throughout your classroom and school.
- Hang positive pictures of people from other cultures throughout your classroom and school.
- Do home visits and observe students with their families.
- Discuss current events, histories, and literature through the lens of how it impacts different cultural groups.
- Include class projects that allow students to get to know each other as individuals.
- Ask your students to write about family customs and share with the class.
- Respect the traditions of other cultures and don't make assumptions about their rituals and practices.

Minimizing Whiteness

As your skills in cultural competency grow, and your ability to show *respeto* toward students increases, the next developmental step is to minimize the impact of Whiteness—or dominant culture—on your efforts as a professional educator. Equity coach Jamie Almanzan advocates that we minimize our cultural Whiteness so that our students of color will not feel that something is wrong with their culture. Do you agree or disagree, and why? If you choose to consciously minimize Whiteness, you might try one of the following:

- Have posters in your room of people of color.
- Include the histories of people of color in your lessons.
- Read the literature of people of color.
- Balance the literature with those of people of color.
- Use positive examples from the media of people of color.
- Include other languages in your room/lessons/interactions as often as possible.
- Allow students who speak other languages to read poetry in their home language.
- Ask students about their home cultures, celebrations, foods, and cultural artifacts.
- Do not privilege any cultural holiday more than any other.
- Understand that since White male culture has been privileged, to counteract it means adding more, not equal, parts of people of color and different gender identities.

For example, when Bonnie assigned a research paper on authors to her seniors, she gave them a page of 100 authors with last names and first initial only. Eighty percent of the authors were women, with a sizable number of women of color, so most students in the four writing classes ended up with a woman author to write about. Had the authors been 80% men, no one would have said anything, but to reverse that and have more papers about women than about men caused the students to note the difference in the power differential. Because the women of color authors far outweighed the percentage of women of color authors studied in anthologies, Bonnie tipped the norm away from Whiteness, while also tipping the gender norm.

Cultural relevancy in the classroom becomes powerful when students have the opportunity to reflect on situations that would appear very differently if the races, ethnicities, genders, and other classifications were reversed. What if football were mostly played by Asians and Latinos? What if we didn't call the few movies centered on females "chick flicks"? What if the presidents of the United States were women of color? What if the Senate and the House of Representatives were not made up primarily of White men? These scenarios seem remote and perhaps laughable, but diverse cultural groups submit each day to dominant White culture—what if it were turned upside down?

When students have the opportunity to consider difference as normal—and see teachers embracing diversity daily in the classroom—learning becomes more relevant for students. Diverse students do not need to see themselves personally represented in every moment of instruction and learning. But it is critical that each student knows that he or she will see him- or herself predictably and as part of the overall learning fabric of the school. As students come to intrinsically know that schooling represents each of them personally and their individual needs and interests, engagement increases, achievement soars, and equity becomes evermore an attainable reality.

EQUITABLE CULTURE IN ACTION: CHAPTER 5, RELEVANCY

In the Equity 101 group on PD360, watch the video segment titled "Experiential Learning" from the program *Equity and Innovation: West Hawai'i Explorations Academy.* This video segment describes the relevancy in learning students experience in their projects at WHEA. In the Equity 101 group, you will also find additional resources to deepen and extend your understanding of equity.

Equity Discussion

Online conversations: Describe the relevancy of your school curriculum and practices. How aligned is the culture and instruction of the school with the background, characteristics, and interests of

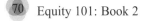

the students? How do the relationships within the school reflect the values, cultures, assumptions, and beliefs of students and their community? In what culturally relevant ways does the school engage all students, socially and intellectually? How does the school culture support relevancy for each and every student? What works, what doesn't, and what is being done to develop relevancy for all students?

Equity Lens: Professional

Describe your professional challenges to relevancy in practice in your school.

_____

_____

EQUITY ACTION #1

Which challenges might you address first? What actions might you take?

_____

_____

In this chapter, you examined the culture of relevancy that exists in the schools described throughout the chapter. In the next chapter, we examine the power of meaningful relationships and the impact they have on school culture and the academic achievement of all students.

CHAPTER 6

Equitable Culture
Relationships

66 I think everybody here thrives on relationship," says Cary Walker, a teacher at J. Erik Jonsson Elementary School. Truly, equitable school culture only works with effective relationships among staff, students, parents, and the community. Relationships are the grease that allow everything else—expectations, rigor, and relevancy—to work. Equity in education cannot be achieved alone, as it requires the collective effort of every stakeholder over the course of the child's education. Without effective relationships, the trust necessary to achieve equity does not exist. With strong collaborative relationships in the school environment, a culture of excellence and achievement develops, thus impacting every student.

Relationships support all components of an effective school culture. In successful schools, collaboration focuses on teachers, students, and administrators learning together; it also focuses on mutually supportive relationships with the community. By collaborating together, the school and the community can successfully build a school culture that guarantees success for all students. What about your school? Does it build collaborative relationships among staff, students, and the community? Or are there too many isolated efforts leading to disparate results? As you think about the quality of your school's relationships, the impact this has on the success of your school becomes evident.

Effective relationships are where the work to create an equitable school culture transitions from technical tinkering to real-world

application. The impact of relationships are seen in both the learning culture and cultural competency of your school:

- In an effective and safe learning culture, relationships not only create but also sustain the necessary affective environment so students can quickly believe the teacher's high expectations and willingly engage with the rigorous curriculum.
- As educators become culturally competent, they become far more effective in developing personally connected relationships that honor the trust and reflect the mutual knowledge developed within effective teacher–student relationships.

Relationships help the student believe in the teacher's high expectations, engage with the rigorous curriculum, and respond to the relevancy of the learning. Effective relationships empower the student, the teacher, the parent, the administrator, and the community. They allow educators to collaborate and develop cultural proficiency, while providing parents, community members, and especially students with a trusted partner in the student's academic growth and development.

EQUITABLE CULTURE: DEVELOPING RELATIONSHIPS

Relationships are the glue of school culture. Working with a staff that possesses positive relationships among colleagues, a principal can accomplish much; however, leading a staff where relationships are not of primary importance sets a course for disaster. Despite all other good intentions, when educational leaders struggle to create and sustain positive stakeholder relationships, all other efforts risk failing.

To illustrate, consider the cases of two first-year principals:

- Principal A, Dr. Smith, is a "just get it done" person who implements a ton of new professional development, bringing in "experts" and generously offering all kinds of opportunities for her staff. Unfortunately, the staff members don't really know their new principal, or her philosophy and expectations. They end up feeling overwhelmed and sabotage the principal through their passive-aggressive behavior: They smile to her face and talk behind her back.

- Principal B, Dr. Hogan, makes building relationships with her staff, students, families, and community her priority. Even though she is well aware of what must be done academically, she does it from the inside out. She purposely develops positive relationships with her staff, students, families, and community, listening to their wants and needs, and then analyzing how the data stand up to expressed expectations. She then structures professional development based on what she heard and what the data show her.

Sandy Nobles, principal of J. Erik Jonsson Community School in Dallas, Texas, is like Principal B in that she came to a new school with a mission, but she didn't drive her teachers into a state of exhaustion. Instead, she focused on building relationships, listening to others, and responding to the community. Staff professional development needs were met with job-embedded, ongoing, collaborative work.

Her teachers responded, acknowledging the necessity for a positive school culture that fosters positive relationships and connections to the community. Teacher Cary Walker comments, "I think everybody here thrives on relationship . . . When you walk in a classroom and you see a morning meeting or just the way people interact with people, I think relationship is number one."

Furthermore, since Jonsson Community School is a laboratory school, there is a strong culture of innovation, creativity, and flexibility focused on figuring out how to drive high achievement with all students. For these efforts to succeed, a relationship-based culture of trust and support is critical. Teacher Elizabeth Desiderato describes how strong relationships are a two-way deal when driving innovation:

> So if your brain isn't made that way to try new things, be a risk taker, if you're afraid to make a mistake, maybe this isn't the place for you. I think [the culture is] why the school has been so successful.

EQUITABLE CULTURE: STUDENT RELATIONSHIPS

Students feel safe to stretch and learn when they clearly understand what is expected of them—and know that it is consistently and fairly applied. Students will rise to whatever actual expectation we have of them. Thus, when rules and standards are unclear, students will often only reach the low bar that has been set for them. But when expectations are rigorous and relevant, clearly laid out, and explained, students will typically reach them. In this situation, the teacher–student relationship is strengthened since the student trusts the teacher to consistently provide the necessary support needed to succeed.

Successfully being part of a classroom community means following the procedures or "hidden rules" of the group, learning what is accepted and what is not. The reason these guidelines are often called "hidden rules" is because they are not always explicitly stated, which requires the students to decipher on their own what matters and what does not, both to the teacher and to other students. If a student does not know to respond, "Yes, ma'am," or "Yes, sir," to a teacher and simply responds, "Yeah," but the teacher sees the formality as an important show of respect, then the student is put in an unintended disadvantage compared to other students who enter the classroom using this formality. Providing clear expectations and routines allows the student to trust the teacher, rather than guarding engagement and second-guessing his or her relationship with the teacher.

At Jonsson Community School, all teachers engage in a Morning Meeting where students are greeted and individually acknowledged, and where expectations, calendar items, and other needs are reviewed. Teacher Katie Cotton describes Morning Meetings as centrally important in establishing routines and building relationships: "Every day usually starts off the same. We have the same procedure routines. I think that when you establish routines the kids know what to expect and they are just so much more comfortable." With comfort on the part of the student comes a feeling of being accepted and heard, and this elementary school's staff works hard to build relationships with all involved.

Sandy Nobles further describes the importance of routines like this:

> Morning Meetings have been in existence in schools for a long time. I know teachers can feel overwhelmed with constraints of time, but I think . . . every child needs to have that sense in the morning that first they've been greeted by their teacher, second that their voice is in the room.

Since equitable culture can only exist with strong relationships between teacher and student, and between student and student, the power of each individual's voice needs to be present and honored regularly in the classroom. And when individuals feel heard and understood, they feel a part of the community.

The Morning Meeting at Jonsson stands as an exemplar of a deliberate and daily process to engage each and every student, and strengthen relationships within the classroom and school community. In the dialogue that follows, teachers at Jonsson describe daily routines within these meetings. Notice how all students are individually acknowledged and engaged daily through this process:

Teacher Cary Walker: It basically started with getting together in greeting. So [students] definitely have choices about how they greet each other. Every morning we greet our kids at the door. And then [students] also greet each other at morning meetings. We have different processes for that. And then at that point everybody has opportunities to share every day. We switch that up. So kids have the opportunity to share and then ask questions and comment on each other. And then, depending on the day, it might be a team building activity.

Teacher Talitha Kiwict: Teachers choose activities that they are comfortable with, and so every teacher has their own style. But the process and procedure of having a morning meeting is the same across the school. And having meetings in general—problem solving is a big component in our classrooms. The whole issue of discipline and problem solving really puts the students in charge of what's happening. It also makes them accountable for what decisions they're making, and how they are going to take the next step to resolve whatever the issue is.

Teacher Elizabeth Desiderato: Really the philosophy of Morning Meeting goes throughout the day. I can't really say that's the only time that my children have the opportunity to share, have an opinion, be engaged, or really interact. It's constant. It's the whole philosophy of "you have a job here: it's being a part of the classroom," saying "this is our classroom, it's not mine."

Teacher Kathlyn Lehner: It starts the day on a positive note as well. It shows them we're all here and ready to learn. We revisit it frequently.

When we belong to a group that makes us feel welcome, we typically experience some of these behaviors between group members:

- Greeting each other warmly with a smile and eye contact
- Asking questions about what has happened recently in each other's lives
- Listening intently with both mind and body language
- Asking probing questions to demonstrate each other cares
- Honestly sharing each other's personal lives
- Sitting together and wanting to be in each other's presence
- Warmly saying good-bye and letting each other know how happy we will be to see each other again

These actions seem like simple things: greet, listen, share, engage, respect, reflect, and acknowledge. But how often are these actions a predictable and regular part of every school day for students and teachers alike? When interactions in the educational environment are treated as true and sincere relationships, collective energy and purpose become the daily norm. When educators do the following things with students each day, they create an inclusive and powerful learning environment:

- Greet students at the door.
- Listen to their stories.
- Share something personal.
- Keep close to them as they learn.
- Respect their brain's functioning by allowing time for thinking, talking, writing, and processing.
- Reflect on the student's learning output.
- Give feedback to the learning.
- Acknowledge each and every student by telling them good-bye, letting them know they are anxious to see them again the next day, and that they are aware and responsive to the learners' needs.

Child or adult, we all respond to this paradigm of learning. Brain to brain, we can feel safe in this environment when the teacher and other students all respond in kind. Relationships are the grease that allows the other functions of the school to succeed.

EQUITABLE CULTURE: COLLABORATION

In an equitable school culture, relationships need to go beyond just friendship to effective collaboration. Effective relationships translate to necessary mutual support, but when lifted to the level of collaborating together toward a common goal, relationships empower action and progress.

As discussed in Chapter 5, when we show *respeto* to others, we honor them and what they bring. When we honor and value others in this regard, we listen to them and develop mutual respect—a strong platform for collaboration. Collaboration works when everybody appreciates the role they play in student achievement and modifies what they do to serve the mission of the school.

Strong relationships build successful collaborations, and successful schools begin their collaboration with relationships. Schools succeed based on the collaborative relationships they foster, both academically and personally. Learning occurs when the teacher–student relationship is established and strengthened every day. Teachers realize they can't do it alone, and once the trust and relationships are established, they find ways to do it together.

Of course, sufficient time to collaborate is always an issue. Once the impact of collaboration is valued, however, creative teachers will find ways to plan throughout their school day. Beyond necessary formal collaboration time, educators learn to use their time more judiciously, talking in the halls, sharing lunch together, and transitioning typical planning time into collaborative sessions. Soon, the routine of sharing becomes the norm, and teachers accomplish more teaming and collaboration within existent school structures.

As with any effort to build an equitable school culture, collaboration requires deliberate effort. This deliberate effort looks different depending on the school site. One school might have a social committee to carry out the suggestions that follow. Another school might have one or two committed teachers who will take them on. In some schools, it might be parents/guardians. Suggestions for building collaborative relationships among staff include the following:

1. Celebrate staff birthdays.

2. Create school rituals.

3. Drop positive notes into staff mailboxes.

4. Start a "Congratulations" e-mail chain where a teacher or administrator writes a positive note to someone in the school, and it goes out to all staff members.

5. Begin staff meetings by sharing positive things about the staff.

6. Surprise staff with a chair massage on staff work days.

7. Create a pleasant staff room for collaboration.

8. Have parents bring family dishes for a special staff luncheon.

9. Set up a cadre of volunteers to help staff with menial tasks.

10. Set up a cadre of volunteers to help staff work with students in small groups.

11. Say, "Hi," each time you see a staff member—too many teachers tell us their administrators walk right by them in the halls without acknowledging them.

12. Get local businesses to donate services, gifts, and coupons for staff.

13. Set up a one-on-one discussion with staff members and meet with each one once a month.

14. If an administrator, do a "walkthrough" each day. At mid-morning, walk through each staff member's room and acknowledge the teacher and the students. Amazing benefits come from making this a daily routine!

15. Add humor to your staff meetings, your faculty room, your classrooms, and your hallways.

16. Approach the most unapproachable staff member and ask him/her for advice on creating a more pleasant school culture.

17. Implement fitness classes for staff such as yoga, hooping, Zumba, and others.

18. Celebrate, celebrate, celebrate!

"Collaboration is really what sets us apart," says Jonsson Community School Principal Sandy Nobles. Her staff member, Anne

Mechler, says, "Everybody works together and it's just a community that works." Sandy describes that at Jonsson, "A teacher comes here knowing that collaborating with everyone is an expectation. That's how we'll learn together and make positive changes for all of our boys and girls. I think that bleeds over into how we work with families."

EQUITABLE CULTURE: PARENT AND COMMUNITY RELATIONSHIPS

In a school that values collaborative relationships, the staff know that collaboration goes beyond working with other staff members. It also means that deliberate collaborative efforts exist between staff and the community, families, parents, and caretakers of students. If relationships are the grease that allows expectations, rigor, and relevance to function, then parents and community provide the knowledge and encouragement that this "grease" depends on. Equitable school culture values relationships beyond the walls of the building because a student's achievement depends on all resources being aligned to his or her success.

At J. Eric Jonsson Community School, there is a prominent wall that is visible to all who enter. It is labeled "Parents/Padres" and is surrounded by student work, thus making the statement that student work and success is intrinsically bound to the families of the students. The families are an integral part of the school community, and as parent Yesika Medina explains,

It's a community school. It's a community. It's not just for the students also for the parents . . . you enter the door and the first person in front will say, "Good morning, how are you?" They know our names which is great . . . and you feel a part of it.

Parent Dolores Ovalle adds, "The children, the students, they treat each other as brothers and sisters—as family."

Sandy sums up the school's relationships with parents by describing,

It is a very inclusive environment. We want families to learn how to meet new families. . . . And so it's a way that everybody is learning it together. Everybody is learning to be honest and authentic with each other and openly talk about our kids. And when you talk about our kids, it's easy for families to relate to each other.

Teacher Talitha Kiwict adds, "Parents are very welcome in our building . . . because they're part of the partnership."

Mutual respect for parents is shown in numerous ways: Parents are included on school committees and councils; educators use the first language of the parents when communicating with them; every staff member does home visits; and the school annually revises an elementary goals plan for each child that outlines the parent's dreams for his or her son or daughter from kindergarten through the end of elementary school.

Principal Nobles builds these relationships by relying on the assistance of parents in multiple unique ways:

Our cafeteria is run very differently . . . Our moms and dads have the responsibility to serve meals [and] they have to serve twelve meals a year . . . It's a way for them to interact with kids [and] it's an interesting way to build relationships with families . . . We all work together in an environment of respect.

This builds relationships and fosters collaboration. Bernice Elias, a parent, shares that the Parents Serve Lunch program is "really good because I get to see my kids at school and they get excited when they see me . . . I get to see what they eat, and I get to see if they eat or not."

FAMILY CENTERS

"Parent," "Guardian," or "Family Centers" are often found in equitable schools where parents, guardians, and community members can congregate and share their joys, concerns, and ideas. Even in schools serving disadvantaged communities, volunteer parents typically staff these centers, offering other family members refreshments and opportunities for collaborating in their child's school. There is often a library of books of interest to families, as well as other support materials and items of interest. There may even be, as observed in a school in a high-poverty area, a closet of clothes and coats to give away to children who need them.

When these centers are warm and welcoming, parents participate, congregate, and collaborate with the school. The room can be decorated like a coffee shop or a garden room so as to appeal to adults. The money to create these parent centers may come from various sources: vending machines, local or state grants, business donations, community donations, and families themselves. At one school, a local furniture store donated furniture for a center; at another, a food supplier gave free coffee/tea for the year. With a little imagination and creativity (and you can bet some of your parents can provide this), you can equip a center for your parents/guardians that will welcome them into your school and build collaboration with the entire community.

Sandy Nobles and her staff opened a Parent Center at J. Eric Jonsson Community School, a place where parents had a "place of their own." In the Parent Center are resource materials in both English and Spanish, and computers where families can access information. The home language of the families is honored in several ways: All meetings are translated, and any information that goes home is in both languages, showing a level of respect and honor for the home language and culture. There is even a station for toddlers to play. They may use the parent center any time of the day, and it has become a real meeting place for families. Parent Yesika Medina says the Center is a great place to go because "you can talk about how you feel and how your kids are doing" with other parents. Parent Rosa Morales says the Parent Center is "like home."

In the Webster Groves School District, in Webster Groves, Missouri, a new male principal in a largely African American community went to the Black churches to build collaboration between the school and the church communities. When he had his first Open House (which had few participants in previous years), he found a room full of community members. He had reached out, changed his behavior, and gone to the community, rather than expecting the community to reach out first to him.

Responding to desperate community needs, Ray Chavez, principal of Apollo Middle School in Tucson, set up a Community School where any member of the community can learn about computers, take English-language classes and classes in other academic areas, and exercise. His College Academy for Parents, which lasts for nine weeks, is a place where parents learn how to save for tuition, how to apply to colleges, and other things needed to support their children. Parents also visit local universities. These initiatives go beyond the school walls and are changing the community. Another initiative that reaches into the community is the AATTACC Club (*Ambitious Apollo Teens Taking Action Caring for Communities*), which is a way for students to perform community service while challenging stereotypes and perceptions of Apollo Middle School students. Student projects have included things such as graffiti cleanup, raising money through activities, and donating to needy causes. Tammy Christopherson, a teacher at Apollo Middle School, proudly states that "The whole school has helped change the whole neighborhood."

In all of these examples, the school members reach out to parents and the community, and modify their own assumptions and practices so that parents engage with the school. Some parents/ guardians are not comfortable coming to school. This does not represent a disinterest in their child's academic experience. Rather, it represents that the parent may not naturally feel comfortable and understand the social norms of the school. If this is the case, educators need to make the first move and meet families where they are most comfortable. This might mean having the meeting in a church hall or tribal center near their home, in a community center or library in their community, or in a coffee shop.

Whatever it takes to form that collaborative relationship with the parent will pay off later in the child's achievement. Numerous studies have found that when parents unite with us as educators, the child has a much better chance of excelling in our classrooms. There are many ways to engage and connect with families through culturally responsive strategies, including the following:

1. Respect all voices and bridge language barriers. Send school paperwork home in English and in the families' home languages.

2. Develop and sustain a welcoming and supportive community for families.

3. Provide opportunities for parents/caregivers to develop skills.

4. Ask parents to volunteer to be part of the actual school day: serving meals, tutoring students, monitoring physical breaks, and so on.

5. Establish a Parent Center.

6. Offer English as a Second Language classes for adults.

7. Create a Community School using the school facilities and resources where parents can learn how to use computers and the Internet, access social services, cook healthy meals, exercise, and attend other classes.

8. Start a College Academy for Parents that teaches families how to apply for and get into college, access financial aid, visit campuses, and practice life skills that show college and career readiness.

9. Have a Family Treasures Night and invite families to bring and share a special dish from their culture.

10. Have an Oral History Night and ask parents and grandparents to come and share their stories.

11. Mutually hold a school rummage sale, car wash, bake sale, picnic, and so on, that is ran collaboratively by parents and teachers.

12. Hold a schoolwide book club for families. Offer it in more than one language. For example, *The House on Mango Street* is available both in Spanish and in English.

13. Create a School Families Album. Invite families to share a family picture for the album which can be displayed in the school library or the Family Center.

14. Create a school garden and have families tend the garden. Celebrate with a dinner with food from the garden.

When all stakeholders—teachers, administrators, students, parents, local leaders, and community members—collaborate together, true equitable school culture can be built. This chapter focused on the building of relationships between these various stakeholders. This is often minimized when staffs address school culture, yet it is a critical component to the collaborative relationships, which must exist for a school to be successful. Considering the powerful results of equitable schools like J. Eric Jonsson Community School and Apollo Middle School, the impact of strong relationships in an educational setting are obvious.

EQUITABLE CULTURE IN ACTION: CHAPTER 6, RELATIONSHIPS

In the Equity 101 group on PD360, watch the video segment titled "A Strong Foundation" from the program *Equity and Innovation: J. Erik Jonsson Community School.* This video segment describes the how the Jonsson Community School drives academic excellence through strong relationships. In the Equity 101 group, you will also find additional resources to deepen and extend your understanding of equity.

Equity Discussion

Online conversations: Describe the relationships in your school.

Relationships: In what ways does your school build collaborative relationships with staff, students, and the community? How does the school support students and educators alike in feeling safe to take risks and stay motivated to succeed?

How does the culture of your school foster or not foster relationships among staff and among students? What works, what doesn't, and what is being done to develop a culture of meaningful relationships?

Equity Lens: Professional

Describe your professional challenges to improving the relationships among students and among staff in your school.

_____

_____

EQUITY ACTION #1

Which challenge might you address first? What actions might you take?

_____

_____

CHAPTER 7

Equitable Culture

Actualization

The goal of equity is that every student, no matter who she or he is, or where he or she comes from, can reach an acceptable standard of academic preparation, now commonly referred to as college and career readiness. Despite our best intents, this equitable education is not a given for many students—especially students of color, students from economically disadvantaged backgrounds, and students who arrive at school not knowing English. If the promise of public education is that any student can show up and learn what they need to learn, then we still have a long way to go.

This is not an effort to criticize the phenomenal work performed by dedicated teachers everywhere. Rather, this Equity 101 series is an attempt to highlight the systemic changes needed so that every student can succeed in every school. For this to happen, the culture of schools needs to change. Adequate school culture change will not come just from creating a positive learning environment. Nor will it suffice for educators to just become culturally competent. What is needed is for culturally competent educators to work together in a strong culture of learning. When difference is normed (cultural competence) and academic prowess is assumed (positive learning culture), excellence will be achieved.

Equitable school culture relies on the successful execution of four components:

- *Expectations:* High levels of success and learning is not only hoped for, but also assumed with each and every student in terms of academic performance, extracurricular engagement, and college and career preparation.
- *Rigor:* A standards-based curriculum is the norm in each classroom, forms the cornerstone of all learning experiences, and is personally optimized to provide reachable challenges for each student.
- *Relevancy:* Students personally connect with and care about what is being taught since the curriculum, goals, activities, and resources align with the students' interests, readiness, environment, and background.
- *Relationships:* Collaboration and trust are the hallmark of interaction between teachers, students, administrators, parents, and the community, leading to a mutually beneficent thrust toward excellence.

Removing any one of these components limits the effectiveness of the others. Thus, the execution of an equitable school culture requires the successful implementation of these four elements. Equity is not a distant goal, but rather an attainable reality when the school focuses on building a powerful learning-focused and culturally competent environment.

Chapel Hill, North Carolina, is typically known as a high-performing school district where children of professors and researchers excel and find their way to some of the top colleges and universities in the country. But a significant labor force is needed to support the highly regarded University of North Carolina at Chapel Hill—and this tends to be less-educated Black, Latino, and Southeast Asian adults. Consequently, numerous students of color from disadvantaged backgrounds enter Chapel Hill schools without the same level of parental education and knowledge as to how to succeed academically when compared to their more privileged peers.

Chapel Hill could have easily hid behind the great success of its wealthier and predominantly White student body, but instead its educators have courageously tried to create dynamic equitable environments and school cultures where all students could succeed, whether or not that student fit the dominant norm.

Key to this effort is the Blue Ribbon Mentoring Program, a powerful and well-executed student support program that exclusively serves children of color from lower socioeconomic backgrounds. The Blue Ribbon program is overt about its emphasis on racial identity development and providing access and opportunity for all of its participating students. At Blue Ribbon, expectations, rigor, relevancy, and relationships are the norm for all students—and the academic success of the program stands as testament to its equitable design.

Few mentoring programs can claim equal success: In a program that starts with fourth-grade students and sticks with them through high school graduation, the Blue Ribbon program has achieved over the last 14 years a 100% graduation rate and post-secondary education rate as well! Blue Ribbon can only be described as 100% equitable with its students! According to executive director Graig Meyer (School Improvement Network, 2012),

> Blue Ribbon Mentor-Advocate is targeting students of color who have untapped potential in our school system. And our mission is to identify those students early enough that we can build supportive relationships with them to help them reach their fullest academic, social, physical, and emotional potential over time.

Blue Ribbon team member Lorie Clark adds,

> It's about building relationships and it's about your word that if you tell a student you're going to be there for them, that you're going to help them, that you do that, you fully commit to what you say that you're going to do, and that you have fun, that they reap the benefits—it's engaging and they're learning!

Blue Ribbon starts with students "that are on the fence"—students with promise but not living up to their potential. The mentoring program provides these students with the additional support and guidance they need to stay on track through middle and high school. The goal is to prepare these students to be college and career ready so that the student him- or herself can choose to pursue whatever he or she desires after high school. According to Graig,

> There are too many people who are too quick to lower the bar for students of color and to say, "You know, it's okay if not all

kids go to college. Not every kid in society has to go to college," which I agree with. But I'm not willing to be the person, and I'm not willing for Blue Ribbon to be the program to tell any of our students that it's okay for them not to go to college. I want to keep the bar high.

Blue Ribbon equitably places the burden of success in life on the student by adequately preparing them to face adulthood ready to work and succeed.

Blue Ribbon Mentor Richard Kwok sees his role as a guiding partner with his mentee, Jamison:

I feel like that's my job to just really point out like here's an opportunity you should take advantage of . . . My advice to Jamison was just give it your best shot, whatever it is. So, if you're going to play basketball, give it your all. If you're going to study, give it your all and don't just mess around.

According to Jamison, Richard fulfills the role of a significant and caring adult:

It was like he was my father figure growing up. He was some-body I can come talk to, or just hang out—make you feel better if you're down. He taught me my manners, how to present myself in public, like say thank you or thanks, and not walk away and not look somebody in the eye when I talk to them. He taught me so much stuff over time that it's like I look at him like a father figure.

Jamison's mom Janet Noell continues, saying,

When Jamison got involved with Richard, that's what I wanted it to be, like a big buddy, because his father lives 30 miles away and he's not that close. I'd say Richard is closer to my son than his father is.

Blue Ribbon Mentoring brings together the community, the school, and the family, all focused on the lifelong success of the student. It is an equitable culture where the norm is success within the differences brought to school by the student.

One of the keys to Blue Ribbon's success is the explicit nature with which it addresses race, racism, and racial identity development. Part of the mentor's responsibility is to help students negotiate society at large, which often is quite different from their home culture. "We ask our mentors to both introduce their mentees to other cultures, help them become acclimated to the larger society and to multicultural settings—and to reinforce that student's own culture, so that their family connection remains intact," describes Graig Meyer (School Improvement Network, 2012).

Students don't lose their roots and strength comes from that. We know that for students of color, if they can maintain a positive racial identity and attachment to their own culture, they're actually more likely to be successful in school than if they become detached from their culture.

Parents concur with the strength of Blue Ribbon's identity development program:

Shari Manning: Having that mentor is kind of everything—trying to make the student more aware so they'll be more prepared for life, and what life can throw at you.

Yolanda Renee Thompson: My students are definitely on a road to becoming successful, productive citizens in this world that we live in.

Susan Hayden: I want to see my son Sam graduate from UNC, be an orthodontist, and be able to give back like someone has given to him. And for my son Allen Hayden, he'll go to North Carolina State, graduate, become an engineer, and he'll be able to give back, just like someone gave to him.

"College is absolutely the goal for our students," Graig continues. No matter the career choice of the student—college or technical—Blue Ribbon helps the student pursue a post-secondary education track.

With this deep and abiding hope from that family that the next generation will be the one to get the education that will help them break out of whatever cycle they're in, the cycle of poverty or whatever it may be, [we] tap into the hope right alongside the realness of the struggles, and acknowledge that they know it's not going to be a straightforward path for the kids, it's not going to be easy. (Meyer in School Improvement Network, 2012)

Most students of color feel that to be successful, they have to assimilate somewhat to the dominant White culture of schools by giving up some of their own heritage and culture. Blue Ribbon aims to reverse this sentiment and help students navigate this multicultural world. Graig Meyer continues, saying,

Blue Ribbon Mentor-Advocate is targeting students of color who have untapped potential in our school system. And our mission is to identify those students early enough that we can build supportive relationships with them to help them reach their fullest academic, social, physical, and emotional potential over time. (School Improvement Network, 2012)

With the help of teachers, Blue Ribbon identifies fourth-grade students of color from disadvantaged backgrounds who exhibit a set of three strengths:

- Untapped potential that a mentor with common interests and passions can help the student develop over time

- Student ability to work comfortably with adults outside of their family

- Family willingness to participate and meet expectations of the program

If a student has those three strengths, he or she qualifies for the program. Annually, the program then finds enough mentors to provide one for all eligible students.

When a mentor begins working with a family, he or she needs to enter the relationship with a positive attitude in a strengths-based framework. Graig explains that "You want them to understand that you're not approaching [the family] believing that they need to be fixed or there's something wrong with their child." This relationship serves as the foundation for the expectations and academic rigor that will be driven by the mentee with the student. Graig continues, saying,

Over time, as the parent trusts you and sees that you follow through in your commitments to help their child, they will then start to disclose to you what their struggles are and what the barriers are to their children. And as you learn what those barriers are, with that trusting relationship, that's when that knowledge that you've built up about their personal history comes into play.

At the onset, the mentor makes a two-year commitment to work with the student. Blue Ribbon has determined that it takes about 18 to 24 months for a mentoring relationship to solidify. If the mentoring relationship is strong after two years, it typically can last through the end of 12th grade. Graig explains, "That's why 90% of our relationships go on beyond the initial two-year commitment. Sixty percent of our students have graduated from high school with the same mentor they started with in fourth grade." Parent Susan Hayden describes the benefits of these relationships in that they have

> [b]rought a real change in my household. I have two kids in Blue Ribbon . . . It really changed their life 'cause they found someone that was compatible and someone they could share interest in, and explore all different avenues. And it's changed my life because it seems like we've brought two other families into our family.

Blue Ribbon Mentor-Advocate is committed to developing the child's strengths and interests through core, enrichment, and incentive components. These components include academic support, social and cultural enrichment, college and career exposure, leadership development, and an incentive component in the form of student scholarships.

When a student is identified to participate in Blue Ribbon Mentor-Advocate, the student, the parent, and the mentor sign a participation agreement that includes the following:

- Weekly meetings between the mentor and student

- Communication with the Blue Ribbon staff about how the student is progressing

– Participation in academic support activities

– Attendance at Blue Ribbon group events at least twice per year

– Visiting at least one college per year

– Participation in community and Youth Leadership Institute service projects

– Participation in at least five Blue Ribbon "choice" activities per year

– Communicating with Blue Ribbon staff or school social worker if there are issues or concerns

This plan was created by parents, mentors, and students, and has experienced 100% agreement—one of the reasons the program has been so successful.

The core components of Blue Ribbon include mentoring, advocacy, and family involvement. According to Graig, "We build a set of supports around the parent-child-mentor relationship. We consider that relationship the core of our program activities. And our components that include the activities that those three people do are our core components."

Within the core components, Blue Ribbon has put a significant emphasis on racial identity development. As described by Director Graig Meyer (School Improvement Network, 2012),

The role that race plays is not so much in the structure of the program, but it's in the approach. And so I've learned a lot in this program about how to talk with African-American families, Latino families, immigrant families, [how to discuss] what types of things they want to know, as well as what types of motivational things they respond well to.

As part of this awareness, when a mentor coaches a student, he or she frames things in similar ways to how the student's parents or grandparents would encourage. Graig continues, saying,

If I'm talking to a parent and I'm able to frame things in a way that I know resonates with their value system, their core beliefs, or their personal history, then they're going to be more likely to engage with what I'm trying to do and respond to the request that I'm going to make of them for how we can help their child.

Historically, for most students of color to be successful in school, they have often felt like they need to give up some of their cultural identity to assimilate into the White cultural environment. How to counteract this, however, did not come easy for the Blue Ribbon program. Graig shares his own learning experience:

When I got here, I was tossed into a situation where a fairly large portion of the African American population in town didn't have a good perception of Blue Ribbon. There was some perception that the program was targeting kids and trying to pull them out of their families or out of the community, and not really being respectful towards the community and the strengths that the families had. And so the very first lesson I learned was that I needed to be a good listener, be very respectful to the local African-American community, learn from the elders in that community, and learn from the families about how they thought the school system could help their children the best.

As a staff, Blue Ribbon engaged in courageous conversations about race. After exploring their own biases, privilege, and racial perceptions, they discovered how to modify their program to honor all voices and perspectives—and challenge the dominance of White culture within their schools and program.

In developing this cultural competence, Blue Ribbon staff and mentors became much more adept in understanding the students, their families, and providing support that actually works for each individual student. Graig explains that

Some kids feel that burden more strongly than others . . . we're going to need to take it on more directly and help [them] engage [their] own cultural strengths to give [the student] that foundation to survive that struggle. Whereas other students who don't feel that's a major challenge for them, they will take advantage more of the opportunities we have to working in cultures outside of their own.

The students attest to this honest approach to race and racial difference:

Maggie Piespass: My racial identity does matter to me because it makes me who I am. Looking at statistics, minority students are mainly the ones that are put down and receive negative comments. But my racial identity truly does push me to learn because I don't want to be part of a statistic. When my teacher addresses race, it helps me understand that I can keep doing this—you don't want to be a part of the statistics.

Erika Franco: I feel that I'm a lot more engaged and motivated to learn when my teacher makes me feel visible in the classroom and when she doesn't try to branch me off because of either my race or because I'm not as smart as the other kids. When she acknowledges that I'm there, and just acknowledges that I'm not like everybody else, we move on from that barrier.

Blue Ribbon has also created activities that consistently reinforce the student's own cultures in their lives. These activities include field trips for mentors, mentees, and families to go places or do activities together that are culturally reinforcing and positive in their racial representation, such as a play about the African American experience, or an art exhibit about the Latino experience.

Blue Ribbon also sponsors a student program called *Seeking the Self,* which is an art-based racial identity development program for middle school students. In this program, students engage directly in issues of race and the struggles they face with race at their age range. Students then work with artists to explore and express their own racial identity development. This takes place during Blue Ribbon's annual summer camp, in addition to a curriculum based on critical race theory that has been modified for middle school students. Core to Blue Ribbon's mission, this overt addressing of racial identity development helps its students of color understand who they are, what they are experiencing, and how to be prepared as a person of color in modern society.

Blue Ribbon's enrichment components include academic support, social and cultural enrichment, college and career exposure, and leadership development.

In terms of academic support, every parent and mentor receives each progress report and report card sent home. Graig explains that

Any student who has a grade below a B, even one grade below a B, is required to have tutoring. And so we provide a tutorial at every one of our middle schools and every one of our high schools, and a community-based tutorial in the evenings, so that all of our students have access to tutoring each week.

The next enrichment component is social and cultural enrichment. Blue Ribbon supplements what the mentors do to broaden the students' horizons:

We ask all the mentors and students to come to at least two of our group activities every year. Most come to between four and six. We have some activities that are cultural, like going to a play, going to a professional sports game. But we also have some things that are specifically Blue Ribbon group events.

Every year there is a picnic with the families of students and mentors alike. There is also an annual graduation celebration where college-bound seniors and honor roll students are recognized.

Giving students college and career exposure is the next enrichment component of the program. Starting in the fourth grade, every mentor and mentee pair does at least one activity on a college campus per year. This establishes for students that participation on a college campus is normal. Furthermore, Blue Ribbon has developed a specific high school curriculum for parents and mentors to teach them how to help their student get into college and determine a career path. Graig explains that

The curriculum tells them—broken down semester by semester from eighth grade all the way through enrollment into college—that these are the activities [the student] should do. It's a checklist. And then for every activity, there's a detailed strategy that tells them if you don't know how to prepare for the SAT, here's how to prepare for the SAT.

The final enrichment component is leadership development. According to Graig,

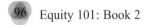

We want all of our students to be leaders and not followers, but also specifically we want our students to be people who are not always the recipients of service, but can be providers of service and giving back to the community.

Beginning in the fourth grade, mentors and mentees are required to do a service project together every year. Student mentee Jamison shares that

Even when we were on our spring break trip earlier this year to Atlanta, we went to a furniture bank. We went to a garden, and then we went to Books for Africa and we had to sort textbooks and children's books. It made you appreciate the things you have.

The service aspect of leadership development strongly centers on the self-empowering aspects of social justice. Blue Ribbon staff member Lorie Clark explains that "It's really about teaching students to care about their community, have a voice, and that they can make a difference, that they can create a movement, and that people can and will listen to their ideas." Student mentee Jamie Salazar concurs:

One of the goals of Blue Ribbon is for the students to get out of their comfort zone. That really helps—I guess it's helped me. I've started to participate more and start doing different things that I probably wouldn't feel comfortable with [before]. I guess that out in the world, you're going to have to be with all people, and different races, and everything. There are going to be times when you are shut down. But from all the activities we've learned, we learn how to ignore it or just see it in a different perspective and get past it.

Expounding on this thought, Lorie Clark says,

I believe you build bridges through race through service. And so when we're engaged in service, no one is thinking about race. They're not thinking about where they live, where they've come from. It's just about our task and accomplishing that task.

Despite all this support toward post–high school readiness, Blue Ribbon does not actively participate in the student's classroom life.

They are strongly allied, however, with Chapel Hill's AVID program. AVID is an acronym for *Advancement Via Individual Determination* and is a national program geared toward supporting middle-of-the-road students who have the potential to make As and Bs, but tend to settle for Cs or below. AVID teacher Corey Waters explains that it is

[p]rimarily a program that focuses on the generation of students who would be the first in their families to go to college. We put together a rigor program in which they are prepared to take rigorous courses in high school, both within honors classes as well as AP courses, before they graduate so that it can move them towards becoming a college student.

Lorie Clark describes some of the college challenges faced by parents and students, and how Blue Ribbon in conjunction with AVID addresses these:

For many of our students, they are still the first generation going to college. And so it's important to do a lot of hands on work in terms of taking students and parents on college visits; learning about financial obligations and responsibilities, such as FAFSA; and helping them complete the college application. But a lot of times, our parents are just reluctant to let their kids go because they are first generation, so it's a scary thing for them. It's more about knowledge and what's going to take place in college.

The goal with the enrichment components of Blue Ribbon Mentor-Advocate is that students learn the skills and go through the necessary experiences that will prepare them for success in college, career, and life beyond their K–12 education.

The final element of Blue Ribbon is the incentive component that provides scholarships to qualifying students. The first type of scholarship is an enrichment scholarship available to students while they're enrolled in the program between Grades 4 and 12. To even the playing field with students from more affluent families, the scholarship allows Blue Ribbon students to take a music or art lesson, go to summer camp, take a class trip, or play on a sports team. Any time these activities have costs associated with participation, students can apply for scholarship funding to take advantage of those opportunities.

When Blue Ribbon students graduate from high school, they are eligible for two types of post-secondary education scholarships:

- The Haidt Scholars Award, which is an endowed scholarship from a local family foundation. Each year, the family places in escrow several thousand dollars to each group of students that start in fourth grade. Blue Ribbon informs the fourth-grade students that they have already been given this money, and that it is in a bank account growing with them. When they graduate from college, the money is divided among all students who completed the program to help them pay for college over four years.

- Sponsor a Scholar, which is sponsored by about 150 donors each year. It is first used to pay for the student enrichment scholarships, and then for post-secondary scholarships. With this program, it supports students who are going to a four-year university, college, or to any type of post-secondary education, including technical and trade programs.

Currently, there are 112 students enrolled in Blue Ribbon Mentor-Advocate in Grades 4 through 12. Seventy-two of these students are African-American, 35 are Latino, 4 are Asian, and 1 is multiracial. Graig Meyer explains that

The structure of Blue Ribbon Mentor-Advocate is all based on research and practical experience about what works best for kids. And in particular, we're looking at examples of what works best for students of color and how to put those things into place.

According to the students, they learn how to let race "inform them" rather than "define them."

Due to its success, the program has grown considerably. When Graig Meyer became the coordinator of Blue Ribbon Mentor-Advocate in 1998, there were 23 students in the program and a $10,000 budget. Today, the program has grown to serve over 200 students with an annual budget of $450,000. Blue Ribbon Mentor-Advocate currently has four full-time staff people, two of whom are funded by the school system and two funded by grants.

There are currently 109 volunteer mentors and 25 volunteer tutors working with the program. Graig explains that

> Our mentors are all over 21 and people who can make a two-year year round commitment and spend at least two hours a week with their mentee. We do not use undergraduate students as mentors because they can't make that significant of a commitment. So we use our undergraduate students as tutors, because they can make it a one-semester or one-year commitment to work with the students. Forty percent of our funding comes from the local school system and 60% of our funding this year is from private sources.

Since its inception in 1995, the program has been lauded for excellence in mentoring and school–community partnerships at the national, state, and local levels. One hundred percent of the Blue Ribbon Mentor-Advocate graduates have enrolled in some form of post-secondary education! Blue Ribbon is a remarkable example of equitable school culture in action. Focusing on relationships as the foundation that allows expectations, rigor, and relevancy to succeed for students in school, Blue Ribbon is providing an enviable future for all the students it serves.

Janet Noell, the mother of mentee Jamison, shares that

> Jamison wants to go to college. He'll be the first in my family to go to college, and I'm really looking forward to that. I am pleased to have Blue Ribbon as a part of my son's and my life. Toward the end of my seven years, my son will get to go to college! Via the parent involvement, Graig has advised me that I have nothing to worry about. All that will come together—finances, how to pick a college. He assured me I have nothing to worry about. Right now, [my son's] in eleventh grade and I'm sort of on pins and needles. I don't really know what to do. I need help right now—I need all the help I can get . . . I think [the mentor's] role is to encourage Jamison so that he can do better than he's doing. He can always excel—he can excel higher than he can imagine.

Her son, Jamison, adds in response to the value of the mentoring program,

[My mentor's] initial goal is to get me to graduate and go to college. I want to go to Rutgers, 'cause like it's my school . . . He taught me that to go for [college], you're supposed to have a good GPA, good grades, and then always try to be good at standardized tests, like SAT and ACT. My goal is to go to college and graduate college!

Considering what Blue Ribbon Mentor-Advocate has accomplished, a simple formula exists for building equitable school culture that can create a 100% learning environment, wherein success for all students can be found:

A positive learning environment plus

Culturally competent educators focused on

Expectations, rigor, relevancy, and relationships

Equals an equitable education for each and every student.

In schools that accomplish this, such as Apollo Middle School and J. Eric Jonsson Community School, educators find renewed satisfaction within their work, parents see that the school has their child's best interests in mind, and students know that success is to be had because they are adequately prepared.

Traditional inequitable schools are like the hard clay in the garden that prevents the plant from blooming successfully. An equitable culture provides the school community and its stakeholders the healthy and progressive environment wherein a guarantee of college, career, and life readiness is assured for each and every student.

EQUITABLE CULTURE IN ACTION: CHAPTER 7, RELATIONSHIPS

In the Equity 101 group on PD360, watch the video segment titled "Blue Ribbon Mentor-Advocates—Every Student—Every Opportunity" from the program *Equity and Innovation: Blue Ribbon Mentor-Advocate.* This video segment describes the equitable success of the Blue

Ribbon Mentoring Program. In the Equity 101 group, you will also find additional resources to deepen and extend your understanding of equity.

Equity Discussion

Online conversation: Describe the actualization of equity at your school. What programs and curricula support equity?

How does the culture of your school support actualization of equity?

What works, what doesn't, and what is being done to actualize equity at your school?

Equity Lens: Professional

Describe your professional challenges to the actualization of equity at your school.

_____

_____

EQUITY ACTION #1

Which challenge might you address first? What actions might you take?

_____

_____

Epilogue

A s you continue examining your own practice and building your skills as an equitable educator and leader, please engage the other three books of this *Equity 101* series, which introduce the Equity Framework and address equity leadership and practice:

Equity 101: The Equity Framework defines equity and introduces the Equity Framework, a powerful model that educators and school systems can use to analyze their own efforts in guaranteeing an equitable education for every student. *Equity 101: The Equity Framework* examines:

- Personal Equity and what is needed to prepare oneself as an equitable and culturally conscious educator
- Institutional Equity and what it takes for a community of educators to overcome institutionalized inequities
- Professional Equity and the necessary practices that educators need to employ to guarantee the success of all students
- The characteristics of an equitable school and classroom: Expectations, Rigor, Relevancy, and Relationships

Equity 101: Leadership explains how to be an equity leader by exploring what it means to actualize equity and drive a school or system toward accomplishing equity for all students, regardless of race and background. Equity leadership requires that formal and informal school leaders authenticate their work in order to truly drive the equitization of schools. *Equity 101—Book 2: Leadership* features:

1. Equity leadership school success

2. Leadership within the Equity Framework

3. Working definition of equitable leadership

4. Authenticating equity leadership

5. Innovating toward equity

Equity 101: Practice develops pedagogical skills that drive equitable practice in the classroom, offering an understanding for why traditional teaching practices actually result in student achievement inequities, and how to replace them with teaching skills, strategies, and pedagogical practices that accomplish true equity for all students, regardless of race and background. *Equity 101—Book 4: Practice* features:

- Equitable practice = school success
- Practice within the Equity Framework
- Working definition of equitable practice
- Culturally relevant classroom practice
- Equitizing classroom management
- Equitizing curriculum
- Equitizing assessment
- Equitizing instruction

We look forward to joining with you in this journey toward educational equity. Please keep us informed of your progress and the successful—*equitable*—practices you implement by joining the free Equity 101 group on PD 360 at www.equity101.schoolimprovement.com. We and other educators will engage regularly with the Equity 101 community online and share the stories of success that emanate from this work. You can also contact us at:

Curtis Linton
Vice President, School Improvement Network
32 West Center Street
Midvale, UT 84047 USA
800-572-1153
curtis.linton@schoolimprovement.com
www.equity101.schoolimprovement.com

Bonnie M. Davis, Ph.D
Educating For Change
a4achievement@earthlink.net
314-496-3596
www.educatingforchange.com

References

Artiles, A. J., & Ortiz., A. A. (Eds.). (2002). *English language learners with special education needs: Identification, assessment, and instruction.* Washington, DC: Center for Applied Linguistics.

Davis, B. (2006). *How to teach students who don't look like you: Culturally responsive teaching strategies.* Thousand Oaks, CA: Corwin.

Davis, B. M. (2012). *How to teach students who don't look like you: Culturally responsive teaching strategies,* (2nd Ed.). Thousand Oaks, CA: Corwin.

Gregory, Gayle, Strickland, Cindy A., & Kuzmich, L. (2006). *Applied differentiation: Making it work in the classroom.* Midvale, UT: School Improvement Network.

Howard, G. R. (1999). *We can't teach what we don't know: White teachers, multiracial schools.* New York: Teachers College Press.

Lindsey, R. B., Roberts, L. M., & Campbell Jones, F. (2005). *The culturally proficient school: An implementation guide for school leaders.* Thousand Oaks, CA: Corwin.

Lindsey, R. B., Robins, K. N., & Terrell, R. D. (2009). *Cultural proficiency: A manual for school leaders* (3rd ed.). Thousand Oaks, CA: Corwin.

Marzano, R. J., Boogren, T., Heflebower, T., Kanold-McIntyre, J., & Pickering, D. (2012). *Becoming a reflective teacher.* Bloomington, IN: Solution Tree.

Muhammad, A., & Hollie, S. (2012). *The will to lead, the skill to teach: Transforming schools at every level.* Bloomington, IN: Solution Tree.

Reeves, D. (2006). *The learning leader: How to focus school improvement for better results.* Washington, DC: ASCD.

School Improvement Network. (2012). *Blue ribbon mentor-advocate helps students of color reach their potential.* Midvale, UT: School Improvement Network, Author. Available at http://www.schoolimprovement.com/resources/strategy-of-the-week/blue-ribbon-mentoring-helping-students-of-color/

Singleton, G. E., & Linton, C. (2006). *Courageous conversations about race: A field guide for creating equity in schools.* Thousand Oaks, CA: Corwin.

Tatum, A. (2005). *Teaching reading to Black adolescent males: Closing the achievement gap.* Portland, ME: Stenhouse.

Terrell, N. D., & Lindsey, R. B. (2009). *Culturally proficient leadership: The personal journey begins within* (3rd Ed.). Thousand Oaks, CA: Corwin.

Video Journal of Education (VJE). (2006) *No excuses! How to increase minority student achievement* [DVD]. Midvale, UT: School Improvement Network.

Index

AATTACC Club (Ambitious Apollo Teens Taking Action Caring for Communities), 82
Academic rigor, 26 (figure), 26–27, 31, 44–55
Actualization, 85–101
Advancement Via Individual Determination (AVID) program, 37, 97
African American students
see Students of color
Almanzan, Jamie, 40, 68
Amherst Middle School (Amherst, Massachusetts), 20–21, 50
Apollo Middle School (Tucson, Arizona), 2–15, 29, 30 (figure), 81–82, 83, 100
Arizona Instrument to Measure Success (AIMS), 13
Artiles, A. J., 40, 103
AVID program, 37

Belief systems, 36–38
Big Hairy Audacious Goal (BHAG), 3, 4, 6
Blue Ribbon Mentoring Program, 87–100
Boogren, T., 103
see also Marzano, R. J.
Bredemeier, Barbara, 49–50
Brittingham, Sharon, 64
Brooks, Barry, 50
Burnout, 40–41

Calabrese, Alicia, 41
Campbell Jones, F., 34, 103
Chapel Hill, North Carolina, 51, 86–100
Chavez, Ray, 2–8, 10–15, 33, 81–82
Christopherson, Tammy, 6, 82
Clark, Becky, 37
Clark, Lorie, 87, 96, 97
Collaborative relationships, 71–72, 77–79, 80–84
College Academy for Parents, 81–82
Common Core Standards, 19, 47–48
Communication styles, 38–40
Community involvement, 10–12
Community relationships, 79–80
Community School, 10–12, 81–82
Cotton, Katie, 74
Cultural competency, 15, 20, 64–66
Culturally proficient communication styles, 38–40
Culturally proficient teachers, 20–22
Cultural relevance, 6–15
Culture of equity, 15
Culture of learning, 20
Culture of relevancy, 62–64

Davis, B., 65, 103
Desiderato, Elizabeth, 73, 75
Detroit, Michigan, 52
Disengagement, 61–62
Diversity, 15

Economically disadvantaged students, 85–100
Educational equity, 18–20
Educator responsibility, 40–42
Elias, Bernice, 80
Elmont Memorial High School, 41
Emotional connectivity, 62–64
Engaging versus disengaging environments, 34–36
Equitable culture
    actualization, 85–101
    components, 20, 34
    expectations, 26 (figure), 26–27, 31, 33–44, 86
    high expectations, 43
    positive learning environments, 17–18
    relationships, 26 (figure), 26–27, 31, 71–84, 86
    relevance, 26 (figure), 26–27, 31, 57–70, 86
    rigor, 26 (figure), 26–27, 31, 45–55, 86
    working definition, 22–26, 23–25 (table)
Equitize, definition of, 15
Equity action, definition of, 15
Equity, definition of, 19
Equity discussion
    academic rigor, 55
    cultural relevancy, 69
    equity actualization, 100–101
    high expectations, 43
    relationships, 84
    school culture, 15–16, 31
Equity framework
    characteristics, 26 (figure), 26–27
    components, 17–20, 18 (figure)
Equity lens
    academic rigor, 55
    Apollo Middle School (Tucson, Arizona), 29, 30 (figure)
    basic concepts, 27–29, 28 (figure)
    cultural relevancy, 70
    definition, 15
    equity actualization, 101
    high expectations, 44

relationships, 84
school culture, 16, 31
Equity terms and definitions, 15
Expectations, 33–44
    belief systems, 36–38
    culturally proficient communication styles, 38–40
    educator responsibility, 40–42
    engaging versus disengaging environments, 34–36
    importance, 86

Family centers, 80–84
Franco, Erika, 94
Frankford Elementary, 64

Gregory, G., 103

Haidt Scholars Award, 98
Hayden, Susan, 89, 91
Hayes, Mike, 20–21
Heflebower, T., 103
    see also Marzano, R. J.
Hidden rules, 74
High expectations
    attitudes, 42–43
    belief systems, 36–38
    culturally proficient communication styles, 38–40
    educator responsibility, 40–42
    importance, 86
Hollie, S., 19, 103
Howard, G. R., 66, 103
Hudson, Tracy, 21

Inclusive environments, 60–61
Indian River Elementary (Indian River, Delaware), 21
Institutional equity, 23, 24 (table)

J. Erik Jonsson Community School (Dallas, Texas), 17, 53–54, 71, 73–76, 78–80, 81, 83–84, 100

Kanold-McIntyre, J., 103
    see also Marzano, R. J.

Kearney, Vivien, 37
Kiwict, Talitha, 75, 80
Kuzmich, L., 103
Kwok, Richard, 88

La Llorona, 7–8
Lamon, Michele, 21
Latino students
   see Students of color
Lehner, Kathlyn, 75
Lindsey, R. B., 29, 34, 103
Linton, C., 45, 103

Manning, Shari, 89
Martinez, Lorena, 3, 4, 6, 8, 9, 10
Marzano, R. J., 29, 103
Mayorga, Kathy, 5–6
McCormick, Michael, 37
Mechler, Anne, 78
Medina, Yesika, 79, 81
Mentoring programs, 87–100
Meyer, Graig, 87–93, 95–96, 98–99
Michigan Education Achievement
   Authority, 52
Minimizing whiteness, 68–69
Morales, Rosa, 81
Morning Meeting, 74–76
Muhammad, A., 19, 103
Muraoka, Curtis, 58

Nakakura, Heather, 58, 62
Nana rule, 5
Nobles, Sandy, 17, 64, 73, 74,
   78–80, 81
Noell, Jamison, 88, 99–100
Noell, Janet, 88, 99
North Glendale Elementary School
   (Kirkwood, Missouri), 39,
   51–52
Northrich Elementary, 64

Olguin, Steve, 8–9, 10
Ortiz, A. A., 40, 103
Ovalle, Dolores, 79

Parental involvement, 10–12, 80–84
Parent relationships, 79–80

Parents Serve Lunch program, 80
PASFUE (Preparing All Students for
   University Enrollment), 12
Passion, 40–41
Perris, California, 37
Personal equity, 22, 23 (table)
Pickering, D., 103
   see also Marzano, R. J.
Piespass, Maggie, 94
Pinole Valley High School
   (Richmond, California), 21
Post-secondary education
   scholarships, 97–98
Professional equity, 23,
   24–25 (table)

Race, definition of, 15
Rancho Verde High School
   (California), 37
Reeves, D., 48, 103
Relationships, 26 (figure), 26–27, 31,
   71–84, 86
Relevant school culture, 26 (figure),
   26–27, 31, 57–70, 86
Respeto, 66–67, 77
Richardson High School (Richardson,
   Texas), 49–50
Rigor/rigorous culture, 26 (figure),
   26–27, 31, 45–55, 86
Roberts, L. M., 34, 103
Robins, K. N., 29, 103

Safety considerations, 59
Salazar, Jamie, 96
School culture of equity, 1–2, 85–86
Seeking the Self student
   program, 94
Self-portraits, 39
Singleton, G. E., 45, 103
Sponsor a Scholar, 98
Strickland, C. A., 103
Student potential, 50–52
Student relationships, 73–76
Students of color, 85–100

Tatum, A., 39, 103
Tatum, Beverly Daniel, 60

Teacher–student relationships,
71–76
Terrell, R. D., 29, 103
Thompson, Yolanda Renee, 89
Trujillo-Johnson, Jennifer,
9, 10

Value systems, 65
Video Journal of Education (VJE),
60, 103

Walker, Cary, 71, 73, 75
Waters, Corey, 97
Webster Groves School District
(Webster Groves, Missouri), 81
West Hawai'i Explorations Academy
(Hawai'i)
academic rigor, 46–47, 54–55
relevance, 58–59
Whiteness minimization, 68–69
Worksheets, 35

CORWIN

A SAGE Company

The Corwin logo—a raven striding across an open book—represents the union of courage and learning. Corwin is committed to improving education for all learners by publishing books and other professional development resources for those serving the field of PreK–12 education. By providing practical, hands-on materials, Corwin continues to carry out the promise of its motto: **"Helping Educators Do Their Work Better."**